INTRODUCTION

Imagine stepping onto the sunlit court, racket in hand, with the quiet murmur of anticipation from the crowd around you. This was the reality for me, who, years ago, could barely hit a tennis ball across the net. From bewildering first steps to becoming the talk of the local tennis community, my journey embodies the transformation we all are capable of. This is not just a story of athletic prowess; it's a testament to the power of mastering fundamentals and building confidence, step by step, stroke by stroke.

You're about to embark on a similar journey. Whether you've never picked up a racket or you've hit a few balls but feel lost in the game's complexity, this book is your roadmap to not just playing tennis but living it. We'll start at the very beginning, introducing you to the essential elements of the game and guiding you through mastering the fundamental skills you need to not just participate but excel.

As the author of this guide, my journey mirrors that of many before me—starting with a mix of enthusiasm and bewilderment, armed with a racket and a desire to learn. My motivation for writing this book stems from my own experiences and the realization that while the journey to mastering tennis is unique for each person, the fundamental steps are universally applicable. I've distilled years of learning, practice, and teaching into a concise guide designed to take you from the basics to a level of competence and confidence on the tennis court.

This book is crafted for individuals stepping onto the court for the first time or those who have dabbled in tennis but wish to take their game seriously. Whether you're 18 or 40, whether you come from an urban or suburban background, this guide speaks to anyone with a willingness to learn and improve. It addresses the common challenges beginners face, from navigating the rules and scoring of tennis to developing the physical conditioning required for the sport. More importantly, it sets out to dismantle the doubts and objections that might hold you back, offering a clear, step-by-step path to not just playing tennis but thriving in it.

You're not alone in feeling overwhelmed by the abundance of information available or the doubts about learning through a book. This guide acknowledges these challenges and is designed to overcome them by offering a structured, comprehensive approach to learning tennis. It focuses on building a solid understanding of tennis fundamentals, improving your skills through practical, actionable advice, and boosting your confidence both on and off the court.

The book is divided into nine chapters, each focusing on a key aspect of the tennis journey—from understanding the game's basics to embracing the tennis lifestyle. You'll learn not just the strokes and tactics but also the mental and physical preparations essential for success. This guide is not about quick fixes but about

A BEGINNER'S GUIDE TO TENNIS

Your Rapid Path to Mastering Tennis Fundamentals and Boosting Confidence

DEREK DROZD

To my wife, my best friend, and my tennis partner for life.
Thank you for being my greatest supporter and always encouraging me
to reach for the stars.
I love you.

CONTENTS

Part One

BEGINNERS – BASIC FOUNDATIONS FOR SUCCESS

laying a foundation that will serve you for a lifetime of tennis playing.

Expect to find a blend of technical instruction, strategic advice, and motivational insights. By addressing specific common struggles and objections, this book offers personalized guidance that speaks to your individual journey, acknowledging the diversity of experiences and challenges faced by beginners.

Each chapter is designed to build on the previous one, ensuring a logical progression that mirrors your growth as a tennis player. However, each chapter stands on its own, offering valuable lessons independently. Whether you choose to follow the chapters in sequence or jump directly to a topic of immediate interest, you will not miss out on any information. This structure ensures you can navigate the content in a way that best suits your needs without worrying about losing the thread of learning as you grow as a tennis player.

As we move from chapter to chapter, you'll notice a focus on not just the how but the why—understanding the rationale behind techniques and strategies enhances your ability to adapt and apply them in real-game scenarios. The book also emphasizes the importance of self-reflection and continuous improvement, encouraging you to see each practice session and each game as an opportunity to learn and grow.

Your journey in tennis, much like mine, begins with a single step: understanding the game's basics. But where it goes from there is bound by neither the lines of the court nor the confines of this book. With each chapter, you'll gain not just skills and knowledge but also the confidence to step onto the court, serve with purpose, and embrace the joy, challenges, and rewards that come with playing tennis.

As we pivot toward the first chapter, remember that this book is more than just a guide; it's a companion on your journey to becoming not just a tennis player but a lover of the game. Welcome to *A Beginner's Guide to Tennis: Your Rapid Path to Mastering Tennis Fundamentals and Boosting Confidence.* The game is on, and it's your serve.

THE GAME OF TENNIS

T ennis, often described as a sport of a lifetime, is a game that combines elegance with intense physical and mental challenges. With over a billion fans worldwide and a history that dates back centuries, it's a sport that has evolved from the leisurely pastimes of European royalty to the high-energy, globally celebrated athletic contest of today.

Tennis is embraced worldwide, with professional tournaments drawing millions of viewers. The four Grand Slam events alone—the Australian Open, the French Open, Wimbledon, and the US Open—attract global audiences in the hundreds of millions each year. The sport is not only a spectacle but also a social phenomenon that connects people across continents, cultures, and languages.

TENNIS HISTORY AND EVOLUTION

The Origins of Tennis

Tennis traces its origins back to 12th-century France, where monks created *jeu de paume* (game of the palm) for entertainment, initially hitting a ball with their hands within monastery courtyards. This early form of tennis, resembling a mix of volleyball and handball, soon captivated the French nobility, evolving into a prestigious sport. By the 13th century, players began using gloves and, later, rackets, transitioning the game from hand to racket play. The game, known as "real tennis," saw significant advancements by the 16th century, including wooden rackets and the construction of indoor courts, symbolizing status among the nobility.

King Henry VIII of England, a fervent enthusiast, helped popularize the sport, leading to more structured rules and the spread of tennis across the English Channel. The term "tennis" derives from *tenez*, the call players made before serving. The modern game of tennis emerged in the late 19th century with Major Walter Clopton Wingfield's development of lawn tennis. He introduced the rectangular court and net play, transforming tennis into the outdoor sport played worldwide today. The first Wimbledon Championships in 1877 marked tennis's transition from leisure activity to competitive sport, broadening its appeal beyond the aristocracy to a global audience. The evolution from an elite pastime to a professional sport set the stage for tennis as we know it, maintaining its core essence through centuries of cultural and technological changes.

Evolution of the Rules

The rules of tennis have undergone significant changes since the sport's inception, evolving to meet the needs of players, spectators, and the game's integrity. These adaptations have helped tennis grow into a faster, more competitive, and universally appealing sport. Here's an overview of how tennis rules have evolved over time:

- **Introduction of Standardized Scoring (Late 19th Century)**

The unique scoring system of tennis, with points progressing from love (zero) to 15, 30, and 40, was standardized in the late 19th century. The origins of this system are somewhat obscure, with theories suggesting it was derived from the face of a clock or medieval French gambling games.

- **The Tiebreak System (1970s)**

James Van Alen introduced the tiebreak system in the early 1970s to prevent excessively long sets. Initially adopted by the US Open in 1970, the tiebreak is played at 6-6 in games, with the first player to reach seven points (and at least two points ahead) winning the set. This innovation made match durations more predictable and viewer-friendly.

- **Changes in Match Formats**

Over the years, match formats have been adjusted for various competitions. Notably, the Australian Open and Wimbledon adopted tiebreaks in final sets, joining the US Open in preventing marathon matches. The French Open remains the only Grand

Slam without a final set tiebreak, adhering to the tradition of playing out the set.

- **The Introduction of Electronic Review Systems (2000s)**

The advent of electronic review systems like Hawk-Eye in the 2000s allowed players to challenge line calls, bringing greater accuracy and fairness to the game. This technology has reduced human error and added an exciting strategic element to matches.

- **Serving and Time Regulations**

Rules regarding service have also evolved, including the foot fault rule and the introduction of a shot clock to ensure games proceed at a consistent pace. These changes have been made to maintain the flow of the game and reduce time-wasting.

- **Adjustments for Player Health and Safety**

The adoption of rules allowing for medical timeouts, heat policies, and the recent introduction of concussion protocols reflects a growing emphasis on player health and safety. These rules ensure that players can compete at their best while minimizing the risk of injury or illness.

The evolution of tennis rules demonstrates the sport's ability to adapt to changing times and technologies while preserving its core elements. These changes have contributed to the game's enduring popularity, ensuring it remains competitive, fair, and enjoyable for players and fans alike. As tennis continues to evolve, so, too, will its rules, reflecting the sport's dynamic nature and its global appeal.

Introduction to Major Tennis Tournaments

The major tennis tournaments, often referred to as the Grand Slams, represent the pinnacle of the sport, offering players the chance to etch their names in history. These tournaments not only provide the most significant competitive stages but also serve as cultural and historical landmarks within the tennis world. Here's an introduction to these prestigious events:

Wimbledon

- **Established:** 1877
- **Location:** All England Lawn Tennis and Croquet Club, London, England.
- **Surface:** Grass.
- Wimbledon is the oldest tennis tournament in the world and is widely considered the most prestigious. Known for its strict dress code, royal patronage, and the iconic Centre Court, Wimbledon embodies the tradition and elegance of tennis. It is the only major still played on grass, the game's original surface.

US Open

- **Established:** 1881
- **Location:** USTA Billie Jean King National Tennis Center, New York City, USA.
- **Surface:** Hard Court.
- The US Open is known for its vibrant atmosphere and modern facilities, including the retractable roof on Arthur Ashe Stadium, the largest tennis stadium in the world. The tournament reflects the energy and diversity of New York

City, offering night sessions that contribute to its unique appeal.

French Open (Roland Garros)

- **Established:** 1891
- **Location:** Stade Roland Garros, Paris, France.
- **Surface:** Clay.
- The French Open is the premier clay court tournament in the world, challenging players with its slow-playing surface and demanding physical endurance. Roland Garros is celebrated for its rich history, iconic red clay, and the unique tactical challenges it presents to competitors.

Australian Open

- **Established:** 1905
- **Location:** Melbourne Park, Melbourne, Australia.
- **Surface:** Hard Court.
- Known as the "Happy Slam," the Australian Open is renowned for its friendly atmosphere, innovative use of technology, and commitment to player and fan experience. The tournament kicks off the Grand Slam calendar and is played on hard courts that facilitate high-speed play.

The Grand Slam Achievement

- Winning a Grand Slam tournament is a coveted achievement in a player's career, signifying supreme excellence and resilience. Achieving the Career Grand Slam—winning all four major tournaments over the course of a career—is an even more remarkable feat, accomplished by only a select few in the sport's history.

The Masters and the WTA Finals

- Beyond the Grand Slams, the ATP Tour Masters 1000 and the WTA Finals also hold significant prestige, offering top-ranking points and attracting the best players in the world. These tournaments, spread throughout the tennis season, provide additional high-stakes competitive platforms that contribute to the sport's drama and excitement.

Each major tournament has its own distinct character and challenges, making them highly anticipated events on the tennis calendar. They not only showcase the highest level of tennis but also celebrate the sport's rich tradition, global appeal, and continuous evolution.

UNDERSTANDING THE RULES

The Court Layout

The tennis court is a flat, rectangular surface with varying dimensions for singles and doubles play. Understanding the court layout is essential for players, as it affects strategy, positioning, and the rules of the game. Here's a breakdown of the key components of a tennis court and their dimensions:

Dimensions

- **Overall Size:** A standard tennis court measures 78 feet (23.77 meters) in length. For singles matches, the court is 27 feet (8.23 meters) wide. For doubles matches, the width extends to 36 feet (10.97 meters).
- **Service Boxes:** The court is divided into two equal parts by a net. Each side contains two service boxes where

serves must land. Each box is 21 feet (6.40 meters) deep and, for singles play, 13.5 feet (4.11 meters) wide.

Baselines and Service Lines

- **Baselines:** The baselines run parallel to the net at each end of the court. They mark the boundary beyond which a ball must not pass on the fly in regular play.
- **Service Lines:** Located 21 feet from the net, these lines run parallel to it and mark the end of the service boxes. The space between the service line and the baseline is known as the backcourt.

Doubles Alleys

- The doubles alleys are the areas between the singles and doubles sidelines. These alleys are in play only during doubles matches, extending the court's width to accommodate four players.

The Net

- The net bisects the court and is stretched across its entire width. It stands 3 feet (0.91 meters) high at the center and 3.5 feet (1.07 meters) at the posts. The net is a crucial part of the court, affecting gameplay and strategy, especially for players who excel at net play or serve-and-volley tactics.

No-Man's Land

- The area between the service line and the baseline is colloquially known as "no-man's land." It is generally considered a strategic disadvantage to stand in this area during play due to the difficulty of returning balls effectively.

Markings

- All lines on the court are 2 inches (5 cm) wide, except the baseline, which can be up to 4 inches (10 cm) wide. The court is marked for both singles and doubles play, with the singles court being narrower.

Court Surface Variations

- The surface of a tennis court can significantly affect gameplay. Common surfaces include grass, clay, hard court, and carpet, each offering different levels of speed, bounce, and traction. Players often have to adjust their strategies and techniques based on the court surface.

Understanding the tennis court layout is fundamental for players at all levels. It informs the rules of engagement, influences strategic decisions, and impacts the overall flow of the game. Whether you're serving, returning, or rallying, a thorough knowledge of the court's dimensions and areas can enhance your performance and enjoyment of the sport.

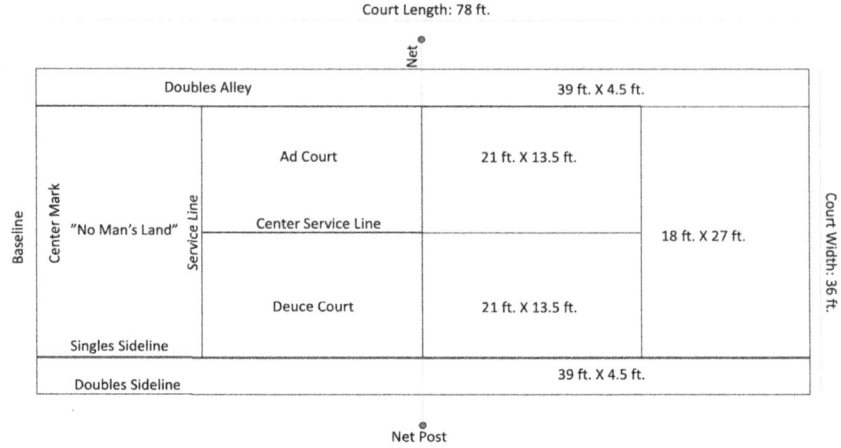

Scoring System

The scoring system in tennis is unique and can initially seem complex to newcomers. Understanding how points, games, sets, and matches are scored is essential for both players and spectators. Here's an overview of the tennis scoring system:

Points

- The basic unit of scoring in tennis is points. The progression of points during a game is as follows: love (0), 15, 30, 40, and game point. Unlike most sports, tennis uses these terms instead of numerical values.
- If both players reach 40, referred to as "deuce," a player must win two consecutive points to win the game. The first point after deuce is called "advantage." If the player with the advantage wins the next point, they win the game; if they lose it, the score returns to deuce.

Games

- A player wins a game by winning at least four points in total and two points more than the opponent. Games are the building blocks of sets.

Sets

- To win a set, a player must win at least six games and at least two games more than their opponent. The standard formats are best of three sets (for most matches) or best of five sets (typically for men's singles in Grand Slam tournaments).
- If the set reaches a 6-6 tie, a tiebreak game is usually played to decide the set. Players alternate serves in the tiebreak, and the first player to reach seven points (with at least a two-point lead) wins the set. The scoring in a tiebreak is numerical (1, 2, 3, etc.).

Matches

- A match is won by the player who wins the majority of the predetermined number of sets (either two out of three or three out of five).
- Special Scoring Terms

  - **Love** means zero or no points.
  - **Deuce** is when both players have scored three points (40-40), and the game is tied.
  - **Advantage** is the point after deuce; the player who wins this point needs one more point to win the game.
  - **Tiebreak** is a special game played to decide the winner of a set when the score is tied at 6-6.

No-Ad Scoring

- Some matches, particularly in college tennis, use "no-ad" scoring to speed up play. In this format, if a game reaches deuce (40-40), the next point wins the game, with the receiving player choosing which side of the court to receive the serve.

Understanding the scoring system is crucial for developing strategies and making in-game decisions. It adds a layer of tactical depth to tennis, as players must navigate the pressures of scoring points at crucial moments, managing the game flow, and adapting their play to secure games, sets, and, ultimately, the match.

Serving Rules

The serve initiates play in tennis and is one of the most crucial aspects of the game, providing the server with the opportunity to start the point with an advantage. Understanding the serving rules is essential for players at all levels. Here's an overview of the key serving rules in tennis:

Initial Serve

- At the start of a match, a coin toss or a similar method is used to determine which player will serve first. The winner of the toss chooses either to serve, receive, or pick a side of the court. From the second set onward, the players alternate serving first.

Serving Position

- The server must stand behind the baseline, between the center mark and the sideline. The serve must be delivered diagonally, landing in the opposite service box. For the first point of each game, the serve is made from the right side of the court to the opponent's left service box (the deuce side). Players alternate sides with each point.

The Service Motion

- The serve is initiated by tossing the ball into the air and hitting it before it touches the ground. The server cannot step on or over the baseline before striking the ball. The serve must be made underhand or overhand, with only one attempt allowed per serve, except in the case of a let.

Faults

- A serve is considered a fault if the ball:

  - Fails to land in the correct service box.
  - Hits the net and lands outside the correct service box.
  - Misses the ball when trying to hit it.
  - Steps on or over the baseline before hitting the ball.

- If the first serve is a fault, the server gets a second serve. If the second serve is also a fault (double fault), the server loses the point.

Lets

- A let is called if:

  - The served ball hits the net but still lands in the correct service box. In this case, the serve is retaken without penalty.
  - The server serves out of turn, and the serve is retaken after correcting the order.
  - A distraction occurs from outside the court; the server is allowed to retake the serve.

- There is no limit to the number of consecutive lets a server can have on a single point.

Alternating Service Games

- Players alternate serving entire games. After the first game of a set, the opponent serves the next game, and this pattern continues throughout the match.

Changing Ends

- Players switch ends of the court after the first game and then every two games thereafter, and at the end of each set to ensure equal conditions for both competitors. During a tiebreak game, players also switch ends after every six points.

Understanding and adhering to the serving rules are fundamental to fair play in tennis. The serve sets the tone for each point, making it a critical skill to master for competitive success.

In-Game Rules (Faults, Lets, etc.)

In addition to the specific regulations surrounding serves, tennis encompasses a variety of in-game rules that govern play and ensure fairness. These rules address how points are contested, scored, and, sometimes, restarted. Here are key in-game rules, including faults, lets, and other considerations:

Faults

- **Foot Fault:** Occurs when a player's foot touches the baseline or the court inside the baseline before striking the serve. This is considered a serving fault.
- **Ball Hits Outside the Court:** If a ball lands outside the designated boundaries of the court during a rally, the player who hits it loses the point.

Lets

- During general play, a let may be called if an external factor (such as a ball from another court entering play) interferes with the point. The point is then replayed with no penalty to either player.
- A let is also called in the rare instance that a serve hits the receiver or the receiver's equipment before bouncing.

The Two-Bounce Rule

- A player must return the ball before it bounces twice on their side of the court. Failing to do so results in the loss of the point.

Hitting the Ball

- Players may hit the ball with the racket, using any part of the racket. Hitting the ball with any part of the body or with something other than the racket is not allowed.
- The ball must be hit, not carried or caught on the racket.

The Net

- Players are not allowed to touch the net, the net posts, or the opponent's court with their body or racket during a point. Doing so results in the loss of the point.
- If the ball in play touches the net during a rally (excluding serves) but still lands in the appropriate court, play continues without interruption.

Player Conduct

- Players must adhere to standards of conduct that include not swearing, deliberately breaking rackets, or engaging in unsportsmanlike behavior. Violations can result in warnings, point penalties, or even disqualification, depending on the severity and frequency of the offenses.

Continuous Play

- Between points, players are expected to adhere to a pace of play that doesn't unduly delay the game. The server is given 25 seconds from the end of a point to start the next serve. Excessive delays can result in time violations.

Ball in Play

- Once a point has started, the ball remains in play until it bounces twice, lands out of bounds, or there is a let called for other reasons. Players must be ready to respond to their opponent's shots until the point is officially called.

Challenges and Reviews

- In professional tennis, players have the option to challenge line calls. An electronic review system, such as Hawk-Eye, is used to verify the accuracy of calls. The number of challenges available may vary based on the tournament rules.

Understanding these in-game rules is crucial for both playing and appreciating tennis. They ensure the game is played fairly and safely, with a clear structure that players at all levels can follow.

EQUIPMENT AND GEAR

Choosing the Right Racket

Selecting the perfect tennis racket is a critical step in a player's journey, akin to a musician finding the right instrument. It's a deeply personal choice that can have a profound impact on your game. When choosing a racket, several factors come into play: head size, weight, balance, and grip size.

- **Head Size:** Racket head sizes range from 85 to 110 square inches. A larger head size offers more power and a larger sweet spot, which is forgiving on off-center hits, making it ideal for beginners. Intermediate and advanced players might opt for a mid-plus head size (95–105 square inches) for a balance of power and control, while experienced players may prefer a smaller head for greater control and precision.

- **Weight:** Heavier rackets offer more power and stability, absorbing more shock upon impact. They tend to be less maneuverable but can deliver more force without extra effort from the swing, which can be advantageous for players with a strong, steady stroke. Lighter rackets, on the other hand, offer greater maneuverability, allowing for quick adjustments and swift swings, which is beneficial for players with a more aggressive playing style.

- **Balance:** Rackets are categorized as head-heavy, head-light, or evenly balanced. Head-heavy rackets provide extra power on swings without the additional weight, making them suitable for those who play from the baseline and prefer groundstrokes. Head-light rackets offer better control and are easier to handle at the net, making them a good choice for players with a serve-and-volley style. Evenly balanced rackets provide a middle ground, offering a blend of power and maneuverability.

- **Grip Size:** A proper grip size allows for comfortable handling and can prevent injuries. Grips are measured by the circumference of the handle. A grip that's too small can cause the hand to work harder, leading to fatigue and an increased risk of elbow problems. Conversely, a grip that's too large can hinder wrist action, reduce spin, and also lead to potential injuries. Players should choose a grip size that feels comfortable in their hand and allows for a secure hold during play.

In addition to these primary factors, players should also consider the racket's frame stiffness, string pattern, and material. A stiffer frame transfers more power to the ball but can lead to a greater risk of tennis elbow. String patterns affect the spin and control of the ball, with open patterns providing more spin potential and closed patterns offering more control. The material, typically graphite for modern rackets, affects the racket's weight and feel.

Choosing the right racket is not about finding the most expensive or the one that the professionals use. It's about finding the racket that complements your physical abilities, playing style, and goals. Many stores offer demo programs where you can test different rackets before making a purchase. Taking advantage of these programs can be an excellent way to find the racket that feels right for you.

Ultimately, the right racket should feel like an extension of your arm, enhancing your natural playing ability and helping you to develop your game. As you grow and evolve as a player, your racket needs may change, and it's important to reassess your equipment to ensure it continues to match your level of play and style.

Types of Strings and Their Impact

The choice of tennis strings is just as crucial as the selection of a racket and can significantly influence your playing experience. Strings are the heart of the racket and can affect everything from power and spin to feel and control.

String Material

The primary materials used for tennis strings are natural gut, synthetic gut, polyester, and multifilament. Natural gut strings, made from cow intestine, offer superior elasticity, tension stability, and feel, which translate into excellent power and comfort. Synthetic gut strings provide good performance at a more affordable price point, making them a popular choice among recreational players. Polyester strings, favored by players who hit with heavy topspin, provide durability and a stiffer feel, allowing for more spin and control but less power. Multifilament strings are made from multiple fibers that provide a soft feel and greater playability, resembling the characteristics of a natural gut.

- **String Gauge:** The thickness of the string, or gauge, also affects play. Thicker strings (lower gauge numbers) tend to offer more durability but less playability, while thinner strings (higher gauge numbers) give more feel and spin potential at the expense of durability. Players who break strings often may opt for a thicker gauge, while those seeking performance will lean toward a thinner gauge.
- **String Tension:** The tension at which strings are strung can drastically alter the behavior of the ball upon impact. Higher tension typically results in more control and accuracy, as the strings deflect less during ball contact. Lower tension can provide more power, as the strings have a trampoline-like effect but may sacrifice some control. Personal preference and playing style play significant roles in determining the optimal string tension.
- **String Pattern:** The pattern of the strings on the racket head, either open or dense, can also affect the game. An open string pattern has fewer strings, which can create more spin and power due to more "bite" on the ball and a greater trampoline effect. A dense string pattern offers more control and is often preferred by players who hit flat and want to maintain consistency and precision.

A player's selection of strings should align with their playing style and what they are looking to achieve with their shots. A baseline player who relies on topspin might prefer polyester strings with an open pattern, while a touch player at the net might opt for a multi-filament string with a dense pattern for more control and feel.

- **Hybrid Stringing:** Some players choose hybrid stringing to get the best of both worlds. This involves using one type of string for the main strings and another for the crosses, which can provide a balance between durability, spin, and feel. For example, combining durable polyester mains with softer multifilament crosses can provide durability without sacrificing too much playability.

The evolution of string technology and the variety of choices available today mean that players can customize their string setups to their precise needs and preferences. While pros may change their strings every match, recreational players should consider restringing their racket several times a year, depending on the frequency of play, to maintain optimal performance. It's also bene-ficial to consult with a knowledgeable stringer who can recom-mend the best strings and tension for your game.

Footwear & Attire for Tennis

Footwear is a paramount consideration in tennis, where footwork and movement are foundational to every aspect of play. The right pair of tennis shoes can enhance performance, provide support and stability, and reduce the risk of rolling or spraining an ankle. Good tennis shoes offer lateral support for swift side-to-side movements, while a thicker sole's durability is essential for with-standing abrasive courts like hard and clay. Cushioned, well-fitting shoes, light enough to promote agility but with adequate support, are vital.

For attire, functionality is key across varying weather conditions. Lightweight, moisture-wicking fabrics keep players cool under the sun, while layers are essential for cooler climates to maintain warmth without restricting movement. Rainy conditions call for water-resistant gear, with adaptable layers best for fluctuating weather. Regardless of climate, attire should offer a full range of motion, protection, and adherence to any dress codes. Comfort, breathability, and an appropriate fit are helpful to ensure optimal performance and protection on the court.

Consider visiting Tennis Warehouse and Tennis Express for all your equipment and gear needs.

CASE STUDY: THE IMPACT OF LEGENDARY PLAYERS ON THE GAME

The history of tennis is adorned with legendary players whose contributions have transcended their on-court achievements, significantly impacting the game's development, popularity, and culture. This case study explores the enduring legacy of a few such icons, highlighting how their careers have shaped tennis.

Billie Jean King

- **Legacy:** Beyond her remarkable competitive record, Billie Jean King's greatest impact lies in her advocacy for gender equality and social justice. Her victory in the "Battle of the Sexes" match against Bobby Riggs was a pivotal moment for women's sports, proving their worth and drawing global attention. King's efforts led to the formation of the Women's Tennis Association (WTA), securing better prize money and playing conditions for female players and laying the groundwork for the modern professional game.

- **Cultural Impact:** King's activism extended beyond tennis, inspiring changes in societal attitudes toward women and athletes' rights, making her one of the most influential figures in sports history.

Rod Laver

- **Legacy:** Rod Laver's unparalleled achievement of completing the Grand Slam twice, once as an amateur in 1962 and again as a professional in 1969, remains a gold standard in tennis excellence. His versatility across all surfaces demonstrated the importance of adaptability and all-around skill in achieving tennis greatness.
- **Influence on the Game:** Laver's success across different eras of tennis, transitioning from the amateur to the Open Era, showcased the potential for longevity and excellence in the sport, inspiring generations of players to pursue a comprehensive mastery of the game.

Steffi Graf

- **Legacy:** Graf's dominance in the late 1980s and 1990s, culminating in her "Golden Slam" in 1988—winning all four Grand Slam titles and an Olympic gold medal in a single year—set a new benchmark for success in tennis. Her all-court game and formidable forehand became signatures of her era.
- **Impact on Women's Tennis:** Graf's achievements contributed to the global popularity of women's tennis, elevating the sport's profile and inspiring a more athletic

and dynamic style of play that continues to influence the women's game.

Roger Federer, Rafael Nadal, and Novak Djokovic

- **Legacy:** Known collectively as the "Big Three," the rivalries and achievements of Federer, Nadal, and Djokovic have defined modern men's tennis. Each has contributed to the sport in unique ways—Federer with his grace and versatility, Nadal with his unparalleled intensity and clay-court mastery, and Djokovic with his exceptional resilience and all-court dominance.
- **Elevating the Sport:** Their battles have attracted millions of fans worldwide, pushing each other to new heights and significantly raising the standards of excellence in the sport. Their professionalism, sportsmanship, and commitment to improvement have set examples for future generations.

Serena Williams

- **Legacy:** Williams' powerful game, mental strength, and longevity have not only resulted in numerous titles and records but have also broken barriers for African American athletes in tennis. Her presence and success have brought attention to issues of diversity, equality, and representation in the sport.
- **Influence on Future Generations:** Serena's career has inspired countless young players to take up tennis, showcasing the sport's potential for empowerment and change. Her advocacy for women's rights and social justice continues to impact the tennis world and beyond.

These legendary players have left indelible marks on tennis, not only through their achievements but also through their character, innovation, and advocacy. Their legacies continue to influence the sport's development, inspiring both players and fans to cherish and strive for excellence, integrity, and progress in tennis.

MASTERING THE GROUNDSTROKES

P icture yourself in a memorable match that captivates tennis enthusiasts, where victory is secured not through sheer power or dazzling serves but through the relentless and strategic application of consistent groundstrokes. You meticulously wear down your opponent, crafting each shot with precision and patience, turning what seems like a straightforward rally into a tactical battlefield. Your forehand is a formidable weapon, and your backhand is a reliable stroke under pressure. Each stroke is a testament to your understanding of technical nuances in grip and technique.

As we dive into "Mastering the Groundstrokes," we'll explore how developing a foundation of reliable, strategic groundstrokes can become a formidable weapon in your arsenal, capable of outlasting and outsmarting opponents, match after match.

THE BASICS OF GRIPPING THE RACKET

Mastering the grip is foundational to tennis success. The grip you choose directly influences your ability to hit various shots and adapt to different situations on the court. The way you hold your racket influences the angle of the racket face at contact, the path of the racket through the ball, and, ultimately, the speed, spin, and trajectory of your shots. Let's delve into understanding the different grips and how they can shape your play.

The Impact of Grip on Shots

Here's how grip variations can impact different types of shots:

Forehand Shots

- **Eastern Grip:** The Eastern forehand grip is achieved by placing the base knuckle of your index finger on the third bevel of the racket handle. This grip is versatile and easy to learn for beginners. It offers a good balance between power and control, making it suitable for hitting flat shots with moderate topspin. This grip facilitates a straightforward swing path and a natural racket face angle, allowing for consistent and precise forehand shots.
- **Semi-Western Grip:** The Semi-Western grip is achieved by placing the base knuckle of the index finger on the fourth bevel. It is popular among modern players because this grip elevates the racket head above the wrist, making it easier to brush up behind the ball for topspin. This is particularly useful for high-bouncing balls and provides a greater margin for error over the net. The additional topspin can also create challenging bounces for opponents.

- **Western Grip:** The Western grip places the base knuckle on the fifth bevel, creating a significant angle between the forearm and the racket. This grip is favored for its extreme topspin capabilities, especially on clay courts. However, this grip may limit the ability to hit flat shots and can be challenging to use effectively on low balls.

Backhand Shots

- **One-Handed Backhand (Eastern Backhand Grip):** For the Eastern backhand, the base knuckle of the index finger rests on the first bevel. It allows for a mix of power and control, with the ability to drive through the ball for flatter shots or add topspin. This grip requires good wrist strength and timing to manage high-bouncing balls.
- **Two-Handed Backhand:** Typically involves a combination of an Eastern forehand grip with the dominant hand and a Continental or Eastern backhand grip with the non-dominant hand. This grip setup provides added power and control, making it easier to handle high balls and generate topspin.

Serves, Volleys, Slices, and Overheads

- **Continental Grip:** The Continental grip, with the base knuckle on the second bevel, is versatile and used primarily for serves, volleys, slices, and overheads. It is the preferred grip for serving as it allows for a versatile range of serves, including flat, slice, and kick serves. The Continental grip facilitates wrist snap and pronation— essential for serving powerfully and with varied spins. It is also the go-to grip for volleys due to its versatility and the ability to quickly switch between forehand and backhand volleys without changing grips. It is also ideal for slice shots on both the forehand and backhand sides, as this grip allows for an open racket face, which is necessary to impart backspin on the ball, resulting in a low and skidding shot that can disrupt an opponent's rhythm.

Each grip has its advantages and limitations, depending on the shot type and the situation during play. Mastering different grips and understanding their impact on your shots allows for strategic adjustments in matches, enabling you to exploit opponents' weaknesses, adapt to various court surfaces, and enhance your overall game strategy. Experimenting with and practicing various grips during training sessions will help you become a more adaptable and formidable player on the court.

Finding Your Natural Grip

Choosing the right grip is a matter of personal preference, play style, and comfort. Experimenting with different grips during practice sessions will help you understand the impact each has on your shots and find the one that best suits your game. Remember, the grip is your connection to the racket and, ultimately, to the ball, making it a critical element of your technique to master. Here's how to find and refine your natural grip:

Step 1: The Handshake Test

Begin by holding the racket as if you were shaking hands with it. This intuitive approach often leads players to a grip that feels comfortable and provides a solid basis for hitting forehands. The angle at which your hand naturally aligns with the racket handle can reveal your predisposition toward a particular grip style.

Step 2: Adjust for Comfort and Control

With the handshake grip as your starting point, make minor adjustments to find the balance between comfort and control. Your index finger's base knuckle should rest on one of the racket handle's bevels. For many, this will be either the third bevel (Eastern grip) or somewhere between the third and fourth (Semi-Western grip), depending on the level of topspin you aim to generate and your wrist flexibility.

Step 3: Experiment with Variations

Experimentation is key to finding your natural grip. Try hitting a series of forehands with slight adjustments to your grip position. Pay attention to how each variation affects the flight of the ball, your ability to impart spin, and your overall comfort.

Step 4: Assess Your Backhand Comfort

For the backhand, especially if you're using a two-handed back-hand, your non-dominant hand will play a significant role. Experiment by placing your non-dominant hand above your dominant hand on the racket handle, finding a position that offers both power and control. For one-handed backhands, try adjusting your grip toward a more Eastern backhand position and note how it affects your shot.

Step 5: Consistency and Adjustability

Once you find a grip that feels natural, work on maintaining consistency with it across different shots. A natural grip should also allow for slight adjustments, enabling you to switch to different grips as required for serves, volleys, and slices without feeling unnatural.

Step 6: Feedback and Fine-Tuning

Seek feedback from coaches or experienced players. They can offer valuable insights into how your grip affects your technique and performance. Use their feedback to fine-tune your grip further.

Finding your natural grip is not just about adhering strictly to conventional wisdom but about discovering what works best for your style of play, physical capabilities, and comfort. As you develop as a player, your grip may evolve, so remain open to making adjustments as you learn and grow in the game. Your natural grip is the foundation upon which your tennis skills are built, making it crucial to spend time mastering this fundamental aspect of your technique.

STANCE AND PREPARATION

Mastering each stroke begins with the correct stance and preparation, which lay the foundation for strong, accurate, and versatile shots. Understanding and practicing the proper stance and preparation can significantly improve your tennis game's effectiveness.

Stance

- **Neutral Stance:** This is used when time is limited, allowing for quick execution. Your feet are roughly shoulder-width apart, with toes pointing toward the net. This stance is versatile and suitable for fast exchanges and baseline play.
- **Open Stance:** Ideal for balls hit to your side when movement is lateral. You face the net with your hitting side foot back and your weight on the back foot. The open

stance facilitates generating power and topspin, especially on the run.

- **Semi-Open Stance:** A hybrid of the neutral and open stances, providing a balance between mobility and power. This stance is adaptable, allowing for effective shot-making in various court positions.

Preparation

- **Early Racket Back:** As soon as you recognize a ball coming to your forehand side, turn your shoulders and hips to take your racket back. This early preparation is crucial for timing and allows you to adjust to different types of balls.
- **Unit Turn:** Initiate your forehand with a unit turn, rotating your upper body as a single unit. This rotation helps generate power from your core, reducing reliance on arm strength alone.
- **Racket Head Up:** Keep the racket head above the wrist during the backswing. This position aids in creating topspin by brushing up the back of the ball during the forward swing.
- **Split Step:** As your opponent hits the ball, execute a split step—a small hop that lands as you determine the ball's direction. This readiness position ensures you're balanced and ready to move toward the ball efficiently.
- **Footwork:** Good footwork is essential for positioning yourself optimally to hit a strong forehand. Use small adjustment steps to align your body correctly with the incoming ball. Aim to hit the ball in your ideal strike zone, typically between waist and chest height.

By focusing on the correct stance and preparation, you'll create a solid platform for executing your forehand. These fundamentals enable better shot accuracy, power, and the ability to apply different spins depending on the situation. Practice consistently to make these elements a natural part of your forehand, allowing you to execute this critical shot with confidence under all playing conditions.

SWING PATH, FOLLOW-THROUGH, AND SPINS

Swing Path and Follow-Through

The effectiveness of a groundstroke is significantly influenced by the swing path and the follow-through. These elements determine the ball's speed, spin, and trajectory, making them crucial for players aiming to develop a powerful and reliable groundstroke. Understanding the mechanics of the swing path and the importance of a proper follow-through can elevate your forehand to the next level.

Swing Path

- **Low to High**: For most groundstroke shots, especially those intended to generate topspin, the swing path should travel from low to high. Starting with the racket below the level of the ball allows you to brush up against the back of the ball, imparting topspin. This spin creates a higher net clearance for consistency and dips the ball down into the court, making it harder for opponents to return.
- **Straight Through:** For flatter shots aimed at generating more power and speed, the swing path tends to be more linear, moving directly through the ball's center. This

technique is often used when trying to hit winners or forceful shots that catch the opponent off guard.

- **Inside-Out and Inside-In:** These terms describe the direction of your swing relative to your body and the court. An inside-out swing path occurs when you hit the ball from your body's inside (close to you) to the outside (away from you), typically used for cross-court shots. Conversely, an inside-in path directs the ball down the line, requiring a swing from the inside toward the same side of your body.

Follow-Through

- **Over the Shoulder**: The classic follow-through involves completing the swing with the racket finishing over the opposite shoulder. This full extension ensures maximum power transfer to the ball and is indicative of a complete, uninhibited swing. It's particularly important for topspin forehands, as the upward motion of the swing naturally guides the racket to finish in this position.
- **Across the Body**: In some cases, especially on quicker exchanges or when adjusting for an open stance, the follow-through might finish across the body at waist level. While this follow-through might not always indicate a full swing, it's useful for quick redirections and adjustments.
- **Adjusting for Spin and Power:** The exact follow-through can vary depending on the desired shot outcome. For more topspin, emphasize wrist action and a higher finish. For more power, focus on a more pronounced low-to-high swing path with a firm wrist to ensure the racket head speed is maximized at the point of contact.

Mastering the swing path and follow-through will not only make your groundstrokes a more potent weapon but will also enhance your overall ability to control the ball under various playing conditions. With time and practice, these elements will become instinctive, allowing you to execute groundstrokes with confidence and precision.

GROUNDSTROKE FUNDAMENTALS

Forehand

The forehand is one of the most crucial strokes in tennis, serving as a powerful weapon for dictating play and winning points. It is executed by swinging the racket across the body with the dominant hand and hitting the ball on the same side as the racket hand. For a right-handed player, this means striking the ball on the right side of the body; for a left-handed player, it's the opposite.

Backhand

The backhand, a fundamental stroke in tennis, can be executed with one hand or two, each style possessing its own unique advantages and challenges. The choice between a one-handed and a two-handed backhand often comes down to personal preference, playing style, and physical attributes. Understanding the nuances of both can help players make informed decisions about which technique to adopt and how to develop it further.

One-Handed Backhand

Advantages

- **Reach and Coverage:** The one-handed backhand offers greater reach, allowing players to cover more court and handle wide balls more effectively.
- **Slice:** The one-handed grip facilitates a natural and effective slice, adding variety and defensive options to a player's game.
- **Net Play:** Transitioning to volleys and net play is often smoother with one hand on the racket, as it closely mimics the grip and wrist position used in volleys.
- **Aesthetics and Flow:** Many players and fans appreciate the aesthetic appeal of the one-handed backhand, often seen as more elegant and fluid.

Challenges

- **High Balls:** Handling high-bouncing balls, especially on faster surfaces, can be more challenging with a one-handed backhand due to limited leverage and power.
- **Strength and Stability:** The one-handed backhand requires significant wrist and forearm strength to generate power and maintain stability through the shot.

Two-Handed Backhand

Advantages

- **Power and Control:** The two-handed backhand allows for greater power and control, as the non-dominant hand can add strength and stability to the shot.

- **High Balls:** Players often find it easier to manage high balls with a two-handed backhand, as the additional hand provides extra leverage and control.
- **Return of Serve:** The two-handed backhand is effective in returning serves, offering a compact swing and the ability to quickly block or redirect powerful serves.

Challenges

- **Reach:** The two-handed backhand slightly reduces a player's reach, which can affect their ability to cover wide balls or stretch for shots.
- **Variety:** While not impossible, executing slices or certain angles may require more practice and skill development with a two-handed grip.

Choosing Between One-Handed and Two-Handed Backhands

When deciding which backhand to develop, several factors should be considered, including natural inclination, comfort, physical strengths, and strategic preferences. Young players might experiment with both styles before settling on the one that suits their game best. Coaches play a crucial role in guiding this decision, taking into account the player's long-term development and potential.

Players like Roger Federer and Stan Wawrinka have demonstrated the effectiveness and beauty of the one-handed backhand at the highest levels of the game, while Novak Djokovic and Serena Williams exemplify the power and versatility of the two-handed backhand.

Regardless of the choice, mastering the backhand requires dedicated practice, focusing on technique, footwork, and strategic application to turn this essential stroke into a reliable weapon on the court.

GROUNDSTROKE VARIATION AND SPIN

Versatile groundstrokes can significantly enhance a player's game, providing a strategic advantage and keeping opponents off balance. Understanding the different groundstroke variations and knowing when to employ each can make a player more adaptable and unpredictable. Here are some key backhand variations and the situations in which they are most effective:

Flat Groundstroke

- **Description:** A flat groundstroke is hit with minimal spin, focusing on power and speed. It is executed with a compact swing and a firm wrist, striking the ball squarely for a direct shot.
- **When to Use:** The flat groundstroke is most effective as an offensive weapon, ideal for hitting winners or applying pressure when you have a clear shot down the line or cross-court. It's best used when the ball is in your ideal strike zone, allowing for maximum control and precision.

Topspin Groundstroke

- **Description:** The topspin groundstroke is characterized by a low-to-high swing path, brushing up the back of the ball to generate spin. This shot arcs over the net and dips sharply, making it difficult for opponents to attack.
- **When to Use:** Employ the topspin groundstroke when you need to add safety and depth to your shots, especially from the baseline. It's particularly useful in long rallies, against

high balls, or when playing on clay courts, where the spin can produce a high bounce, challenging the opponent's timing and positioning.

Slice Groundstroke

- **Description:** The slice groundstroke imparts a backspin on the ball, causing it to float and skid upon landing. This shot is executed with an open racket face, slicing underneath the ball in a high-to-low motion.
- **When to Use:** Use the slice to change the pace of the game, for defensive purposes, or to approach the net. It's effective in neutralizing powerful shots, dealing with low balls, and drawing opponents out of their comfort zone by varying the ball's speed and bounce.

Drop Shot

- **Description:** A softly hit shot that barely clears the net and lands softly in the opponent's court, the drop shot is executed with finesse, using a slight backspin to control its trajectory and speed.
- **When to Use:** The drop shot is a tactical weapon, best used when your opponent is positioned deep in the baseline to draw them forward and out of position. It requires precise timing and touch and is most effective when unexpected.

Volley

- **Description:** We will cover volleys in detail in the coming chapters. A volley is hit out of the air before the ball bounces, using a short and compact swing. It requires quick reflexes and is executed close to the net with minimal backswing and follow-through.

- **When to Use:** Use the volley during net play, either when serving and volleying or following up an approach shot. It's a key shot in doubles and an effective way to finish points quickly in singles by cutting off the opponent's angles.

Lob

- **Description:** The lob sends the ball high over the opponent's head, ideally landing deep in the court. It can be hit with topspin to control its depth and trajectory.
- **When to Use:** The lob is useful when your opponent is close to the net, either to pass them or to give yourself time to recover position. It can also be used defensively to reset the point or offensively to catch the opponent off guard.

Mastering these groundstroke variations requires practice and a strategic understanding of when and how to use them effectively. Each variation adds depth to your game, allowing you to adapt to different opponents and conditions, keeping your play dynamic and challenging to counter.

COMMON MISTAKES AND HOW TO CORRECT THEM

Even with a strong grasp of groundstroke fundamentals, certain common mistakes can hinder the effectiveness of your shot. Identifying and correcting these errors is crucial for improving your forehand and overall game. Here are some frequent missteps and strategies for rectification:

Inadequate Preparation

- **Mistake:** Failing to prepare early can lead to rushed shots, poor footwork, and suboptimal contact with the ball.
- **Correction:** Focus on early racket preparation and unit turn as soon as the ball is headed your way. This ensures you have ample time to adjust your position and decide on the best shot.

Poor Footwork

- **Mistake:** Static feet or incorrect foot positioning can result in reaching for the ball, leading to weak shots and limited control.
- **Correction:** Practice dynamic footwork drills to improve agility and ensure you're always moving your feet to get into the optimal position for each shot. Incorporate split steps and adjustment steps into your movement pattern.

Poor Weight Transfer

- **Mistake:** Failing to transfer your weight through the ball can result in a weak and ineffective groundstroke.
- **Correction:** Start with your weight on the back foot, and as you swing, shift your weight to your front foot. This movement should be practiced until it becomes a smooth, integrated part of your stroke.

Incorrect Grip

- **Mistake:** Using the wrong grip or adjusting the grip mid-swing can negatively impact power and spin.

- **Correction:** Spend time understanding different grips and their applications. Ensure a consistent grip that suits your playing style, and practice transitioning between grips smoothly when necessary.

Excessive Wrist Use

- **Mistake:** Relying too much on wrist action can lead to unforced errors and a loss of power.
- **Correction:** Keep the wrist firm through the point of contact to ensure stability and control. The power should come from the rotation of the body and the arm's extension.

Overreliance on Arm Strength

- **Mistake:** Relying too much on arm strength rather than utilizing the whole body can lead to inconsistent shots and increased injury risk.
- **Correction:** Focus on integrating your entire body into the forehand stroke. Engage your legs, core, and shoulders to generate power from the ground up, using your arm and wrist to guide the shot and add spin.

Improper Contact Point

- **Mistake:** Hitting the ball too early or too late can cause shots to go off target or lack power.
- **Correction:** Work on timing drills to find the ideal contact point, typically in front of the body and at a comfortable distance. Adjust your preparation and footwork to consistently meet the ball at this point.

Incomplete Follow-Through

- **Mistake:** Cutting the follow-through short can limit shot power and control, making it difficult to impart the desired spin.
- **Correction:** Ensure a complete follow-through over your shoulder (for topspin shots) or across your body (for flatter shots), depending on the situation. This completes the kinetic chain, maximizing shot effectiveness.

Lack of Variability

- **Mistake:** Using the same forehand shot regardless of the situation can make your game predictable.
- **Correction:** Practice hitting forehands with different spins, speeds, and trajectories. Incorporate drills that simulate match scenarios, requiring you to adjust your forehand based on the incoming shot.

By recognizing and addressing these common mistakes, you can significantly improve the consistency, power, and versatility of your forehand. Regularly reviewing your technique, possibly with video analysis or feedback from a coach, can help identify areas for improvement. Remember, mastering the forehand is a continuous process that requires patience, practice, and a willingness to adapt and refine your technique.

DRILLS TO IMPROVE YOUR GROUNDSTROKES

Enhancing your groundstrokes requires focused practice with drills designed to improve technique, power, consistency, and adaptability. Here are several drills that can help elevate your groundstrokes, making them a more effective and reliable part of your game:

Cross-Court Rallies

- **Routine:** Partner with another player and engage in continuous cross-court rallies, aiming to keep the ball in play for as long as possible. Focus on maintaining a consistent depth and pace.
- **Objective:** This drill improves rhythm, timing, and spatial awareness, which is essential for groundstroke consistency.

Down-the-Line Precision

- **Routine:** Practice hitting groundstrokes down the line, using cones or targets to mark your desired landing spots. Begin with slow, controlled shots, gradually increasing speed as your accuracy improves.
- **Objective:** It enhances control and precision on the groundstrokes, teaching you to maintain consistency while changing directions.

Feeds with Movement

- **Routine:** Have a coach or hitting partner feed balls to various spots on both the forehand and backhand sides, forcing you to move laterally, forward, and backward to hit each shot. Incorporate different backhand types (flat, topspin, and slice) based on feed location.
- **Objective:** This builds footwork and shot selection skills, which are critical for adapting both the forehand and backhand to different play situations.

High Ball Adaptation

- **Routine:** Practice hitting high forehand and backhand shots, either from a ball machine set to deliver high-bouncing balls or from a partner lobbing balls to your backhand side. Focus on adjusting your grip, stance, and swing to effectively manage high balls.
- **Objective:** This improves your ability to handle high and deep balls on both forehand and backhand sides, a common challenge in matches.

Return of Serve Drill

- **Routine:** Work on returning serves to your forehand and backhand sides. This drill simulates match conditions and improves your reaction time, footwork, and shot selection under pressure.
- **Objective:** Focus on returning with depth and accuracy, setting up offensive opportunities, or neutralizing your opponent's serve.

Target Practice with Variations

- **Routine:** Set up targets in different areas of the court (e.g., near the baseline, mid-court, and close to the net) and practice hitting forehands and backhands with the intent to hit the targets. Mix up the routine by including flat shots, topspins, and slices.
- **Objective:** Develop accuracy and control over your forehand and backhand while encouraging the use of different shot types based on tactical situations.

Solo Wall Drills

- **Routine:** Utilize a wall or backboard to practice your forehand and backhand strokes. Aim for consistency in shot placement, and try to hit a set number of consecutive groundstrokes without error.
- **Objective:** Improve muscle memory, endurance, and consistency through repetitive practice in a controlled environment.

Shadow Swinging

- **Routine:** Without a ball, practice your forehand and backhand swings, focusing on proper technique, footwork, and body rotation.
- **Objective:** Shadow swinging can reinforce muscle memory and is an excellent way to warm up or refine your stroke mechanics without the pressure of hitting a ball.

Incorporating these drills into your practice sessions will systematically address various aspects of your groundstrokes, from basic techniques to advanced strategic applications. Consistency comes with time and dedication; monitor your progress and adjust your practice routines as needed to address areas of improvement. With focused effort, your forehand and backhand can become a reliable and formidable part of your tennis arsenal.

CASE STUDY: ANDY MURRAY'S RELIABLE GROUNDSTROKES AND BASELINE PLAY

Andy Murray, the Scottish powerhouse, emerged as a beacon of resilience and precision in professional tennis, carving out a space among the sport's elite with his intelligent baseline play and consistent groundstrokes. Murray's career is a testament to the efficacy of a well-constructed game based on solid fundamentals and strategic prowess. This case study examines the key components of Murray's success and how his unwavering baseline game propelled him to the apex of tennis.

Ascension to Tennis Elite

Murray burst onto the professional scene in the mid-2000s with a game that was immediately recognized for its depth and strategic acumen. His ascent to the top was marked by a series of significant achievements, including winning three Grand Slam titles, two at Wimbledon and one at the US Open, and securing two Olympic gold medals.

- **Strategic Baseline Play**

Murray's baseline play is distinguished by its consistency and variety. He can sustain long rallies with deep, penetrating groundstrokes and is adept at changing the pace and spin to disrupt opponents' rhythms. His ability to play defensively, turning seemingly defensive positions into offensive opportunities, is a hallmark of his game.

- **Reliable Groundstrokes**

The cornerstone of Murray's playing style is his reliable groundstrokes. His forehand and backhand are equally formidable, crafted through years of practice to deliver precision under pressure. Murray's groundstrokes, especially his backhand, are celebrated for their technique and effectiveness, often cited as some of the best in the game.

- **Tactical Intelligence**

Murray's intelligence on the court sets him apart. His strategic decision-making, shot selection, and ability to read opponents' plays make him a formidable strategist. He is known for his tactical versatility, being capable of altering his game plan mid-match to gain the upper hand.

Overcoming Challenges

Murray's career has been punctuated by challenges, including fierce competition from contemporaries like Federer, Nadal, and Djokovic and a series of injuries that threatened to derail his career. His response to these challenges showcased his resilience and determination, continuously working to refine his game and adapt his strategies to remain competitive.

Legacy and Impact

Andy Murray's contributions to tennis go beyond his accolades. He has been a consistent advocate for gender equality in the sport and has used his platform to speak out on various issues, further solidifying his role as an ambassador for tennis.

His legacy in tennis is characterized by his extraordinary baseline game, his dependable groundstrokes, and his exceptional mental toughness. Murray's career serves as an inspiration for players who prioritize strategy, consistency, and mental strength, demonstrating that these qualities can lead to success at the highest levels of tennis. His journey reflects the adage that reliability and smart play can indeed triumph, marking him as one of the most accomplished players of his generation.

Equipped with the skills to master both the forehand and backhand strokes, you've laid a solid foundation for your tennis game. However, no tennis match begins without the initial spark that ignites the rally—the serve. Serving is not just about putting the ball in play; it's a powerful weapon that can set the tone for the point, giving you the upper hand from the very start. As we transition from the nuanced skills of groundstrokes to the precision and power of serving, remember that the serve is your first opportunity to dominate the game. It's time to elevate your play and introduce an element of strategic advantage. Chapter 3, "The Art of Serves, Volleys, and Overheads," will guide you through the mechanics, strategies, and mental approach to these strokes, transforming them from a mere starting stroke to a key component of your winning arsenal. Let's serve your way into the game, mastering the art that can often dictate the outcome of a match.

THE ART OF SERVES, VOLLEYS, AND OVERHEADS

I magine being in a stadium, the air charged with anticipation as two titans of tennis face off in a grueling battle that has enthralled the audience for hours. The score is locked in a tense deuce in the final set, a testament to the evenly matched prowess on display. With the game, set, and championship on the line, you stand tall and composed, bouncing the ball deliberately and eyeing the narrow corridor of opportunity that lies on the other side of the net. In a fluid motion, you unleash a serve—a perfect blend of power, precision, and spin—arching gracefully into the service box and thundering past the opponent's outstretched racket. A game-winning ace in the climax of a major tournament, and the crowd goes wild!

As we embark on Chapter 3, "The Art of Serves, Volleys, and Overheads," we delve into the techniques, strategies, and drills that transform the serve from a mere start to a rally into a dynamic and decisive force in tennis, capable of defining the outcomes of matches and careers.

SERVING BASICS

The Importance of a Good Serve

The serve is the only shot in tennis where you have complete control over the ball's initiation, making it a critical aspect of the game that can significantly influence match outcomes. A good serve sets the tone for the point, allowing the server to start on the offensive and putting immediate pressure on the opponent. Here are key reasons why developing a strong serve is essential:

- **Dominance from the Start:** The serve is the opening move in the chess game, which is a tennis match. A powerful, well-placed serve can dominate an opponent, earning easy points through aces or unreturnable shots. It sets a precedent for the rally, allowing the server to dictate play from the outset.
- **Strategic Advantage:** Beyond power, a good serve offers strategic diversity. Skilled servers can manipulate ball speed, spin, and placement, making it difficult for returners to predict and comfortably return the ball. This unpredictability can exploit opponents' weaknesses or neutralize their strengths.
- **Psychological Edge:** A consistent and effective serve can have a significant psychological impact on both the server and the receiver. For the server, confidence in their serve can boost overall game confidence. For the opponent, facing a formidable serve can be daunting, potentially leading to frustration and forced errors in their game.
- **Defensive Tool:** In tight situations, a reliable serve can be a lifeline, helping to save break points and maintain leads.

The ability to deliver under pressure can shift momentum and alter the course of a match.

- **Foundation for Improvement:** Mastering serving basics is a foundation for overall game improvement. The techniques and body mechanics learned through serving are applicable across various strokes and strategies in tennis.
- **Long-Term Benefit:** Unlike other aspects of tennis that may decline with age or physical condition, a well-crafted serve can remain a weapon throughout a player's career. It requires technique, timing, and strategic thinking, aspects that can be honed and maintained over time.

Developing a good serve involves understanding its mechanics, practicing various serve types (flat, slice, and kick), and integrating serves into comprehensive match strategies. A focus on serving basics not only enhances your immediate game performance but also contributes to long-term development and success in tennis. Whether you're a beginner learning the ropes or an experienced player aiming to refine your skills, investing time and effort in improving your serve can pay dividends on the court.

Types of Serves: Flat, Slice, and Kick

A well-rounded tennis player has a variety of serves at their disposal, each suited to different situations and strategies. The three primary types of serves—flat, slice, and kick—offer distinct advantages and can be used to keep opponents guessing. Mastering each serve type enhances your game, making your service games more effective and challenging for your opponents.

Flat Serve

- **Description:** The flat serve is characterized by minimal spin and maximum speed. It's hit with a direct swing path and a firm wrist, allowing the ball to travel as fast as possible in a straight line.
- **Advantages:** This serve is ideal for winning easy points through aces or forcing weak returns due to its speed. It's most effective when accurately placed in the corners of the service box.
- **When to Use:** Use the flat serve when you want to apply immediate pressure, especially on first serves or at crucial points where a powerful, decisive shot can shift the momentum in your favor.

Slice Serve

- **Description:** The slice serve incorporates side spin, causing the ball to curve through the air and slice away from the opponent upon bouncing. It's achieved by brushing the ball's side at an angle during contact.
- **Advantages:** The slice serve is excellent for pulling opponents wide off the court, opening up the court for the next shot. Its curving trajectory and change of pace can disrupt the returner's timing and positioning.
- **When to Use:** The slice serve is particularly effective on the deuce side for right-handed players (and the ad side for left-handers), where the spin moves the ball away from the opponent. It's a strategic choice for mixing up your serve patterns and for use as a second serve, offering a higher margin of safety than a flat serve.

Kick Serve

- **Description:** The kick serve is executed with topspin and a bit of side spin, causing the ball to bounce high and kick up toward the returner. It's achieved by striking the ball from low to high and across its back, imparting the necessary spin.
- **Advantages:** This serve is challenging to return due to its high bounce, especially on surfaces like clay or high-bouncing hard courts. It can push the opponent far back or force them to hit an uncomfortable, high return, setting up an offensive opportunity for the server.
- **When to Use:** The kick serve is an effective second serve option due to its high net clearance and deep bounce, reducing the risk of double faults while still posing a challenge for opponents. It's also useful in varying serve patterns and targeting opponents' weaker shots.

Developing proficiency in all three serve types—flat, slice, and kick—provides a tactical advantage, allowing you to adapt your serving strategy based on the match context, opponent's weaknesses, and court surface. Regular practice, combined with strategic application in match play, will enable you to wield your serve as a versatile and potent weapon in your tennis arsenal.

Serving Stance and Ball Toss

A successful serve begins long before the racket makes contact with the ball. Two fundamental aspects—serving stance and ball toss—set the stage for a powerful, accurate, and consistent serve. Mastering these elements is crucial for developing an effective serve that can withstand the pressures of match play.

Serving Stance

- **Description:** The serving stance is the position a player adopts just before initiating the serve. It involves the alignment of the feet, the distribution of weight, and the orientation of the body in relation to the baseline and the target.
- **Key Components:**

  - **Feet Positioning:** Your feet should be positioned shoulder-width apart for balance, with the front foot pointing toward the target and the back foot parallel to the baseline or slightly angled. This positioning provides stability and allows for a fluid motion into the serve.
  - **Weight Distribution:** Start with most of your weight on the back foot, enabling a forward momentum as you move into the serve. This forward movement is key to generating power.
  - **Body Alignment:** Your body should be slightly side-on to the net, with your shoulders and hips rotated, preparing for the uncoiling motion that generates serve power.

Ball Toss

- **Description:** The ball toss is the action of releasing the ball into the air before the serve. A consistent and well-placed ball toss is essential for timing and accuracy.
- **Key Components:**

  - **Height:** The toss should be high enough to allow you to fully extend your arm and hit the ball at its apex or slightly on the way down, depending on personal preference and the type of serve being executed.

- ○ **Location:** The ideal toss location varies with the type of serve. For flat serves, the ball should be slightly in front of you and in line with your hitting shoulder. For slice serves, the ball should be tossed more to the side, enabling you to hit across it. For kick serves, the ball should be tossed slightly behind you, allowing for the upward brushing action required for topspin.
- ○ **Consistency:** Practicing a consistent ball toss, in terms of height and placement, is vital for serve reliability. A varied toss leads to timing issues and can compromise the effectiveness of the serve.

Practice Tips

- Spend time isolating and practicing just the ball toss to develop consistency.
- Record your serve to analyze your stance and toss, making adjustments as needed.
- Practice serves, focusing on one aspect at a time (stance or toss) before combining them.

The serving stance and ball toss are the foundation upon which the serve is built. By dedicating time to refine these aspects, players can significantly improve their serve's power, accuracy, and consistency. Remember, the serve is your opportunity to start the point on your terms, making the investment in these fundamentals well worth the effort.

Adjusting Your Serve in Different Conditions

Tennis matches are played in a variety of conditions that can significantly affect serve performance. From outdoor elements like wind and sun to different court surfaces, adapting your serve to suit changing conditions is crucial for maintaining effectiveness. Here's how to adjust your serve in various playing environments:

Wind

- **Adjusting for Wind Direction:** In windy conditions, it's essential to adjust both the power and the placement of your serve. When serving into the wind, you may need to add extra power, as the wind will slow the ball down. Conversely, when serving with the wind, focus on control, as the wind can carry the ball faster and further.
- **Lower Ball Toss:** Consider lowering your ball toss to reduce the impact of the wind, making it easier to time your serve accurately.

Sun

- **Changing Toss Location:** When serving into the sun, adjusting the location of your ball toss can help minimize the impact of the glare. Experiment with tossing the ball more to the side rather than directly overhead to avoid looking directly into the sun.
- **Sunglasses or Visor:** Using sunglasses or a visor can help reduce the sun's glare, improving visibility and comfort while serving.

Court Surface

- **Adapting to Surface Speed:** The speed and bounce of different court surfaces (clay, grass, and hard) can affect how your serve plays. On faster surfaces like grass, flat serves can be more effective, while on slower surfaces like clay, adding topspin with a kick serve can create challenging high bounces for the returner.
- **Adjusting Serve Strategy:** Consider the tactical advantages of each surface. For example, on clay courts, where breaks of serve are more common, placing a higher emphasis on serve consistency and placement over raw power might be more effective.

Altitude

- **Compensating for Ball Flight:** At higher altitudes, the air is thinner, which can cause the ball to travel faster and bounce higher. You might need to adjust your serve by adding more spin to control the ball's flight and ensure it lands in the service box.

Temperature

- **Adjusting for Ball Behavior:** Temperature can affect how the ball behaves; in colder conditions, the ball becomes harder and less responsive, requiring more force to achieve the desired serve speed. In warmer conditions, the ball can become livelier, necessitating adjustments for control.

Practice and Preparation

- **Environmental Practice Sessions:** Whenever possible, practice serving in various conditions to familiarize yourself with how your serve needs to be adjusted. This experience can prove invaluable during competitive matches.
- **Mental Flexibility:** Be mentally prepared to adjust your serving strategy based on the conditions of the day. Flexibility and the ability to adapt are key to overcoming the challenges posed by different playing environments.

Adjusting your serve for different conditions is a skill that develops with experience and mindful practice. By learning to read the environment and adapt accordingly, you can maintain a high level of serve performance, regardless of the challenges presented by the weather, court surface, or other external factors.

Mixing Up Your Serves

A key strategy in tennis that keeps opponents guessing and off-balance is the ability to mix up your serves effectively. Varied serving not only makes it difficult for returners to anticipate and prepare but also opens up opportunities to win points directly off the serve or establish a favorable position for the subsequent rally.

While a powerful serve can be a formidable weapon in tennis, strategic placement often proves to be even more effective in securing points. Mastery of serve placement allows a player to exploit opponents' weaknesses, conserve energy, and maintain control of the game tempo. Here's how and why to incorporate variety into your serving game:

Variety in Speed

- Altering the speed of your serves is a straightforward way to disrupt your opponent's timing. Intersperse powerful serves with softer ones to prevent the returner from settling into a rhythm. A change in speed can force errors or weak returns, providing an easy follow-up shot.

Variety in Spin

- Mixing different types of spin—flat, slice, and kick—adds a layer of complexity to your serve. A flat serve maximizes speed and penetration; a slice serve introduces lateral movement, making it harder to predict; and a kick serve bounces higher, potentially complicating the return for your opponent.

Variety in Placement

- Aim to distribute your serves across all possible areas within the service box: wide, body, and down the T. Varying placements within a game can exploit the returner's weaknesses, stretch their movement on the court, or jam them with body serves, reducing the effectiveness of their return.

Strategic Use of First and Second Serves

- While the first serve is often an opportunity to gain an outright advantage with power or precision, the second serve benefits from strategic variety. Using a kick serve or a well-placed slice as a second serve can keep opponents defensive and limit their opportunities to attack.

Situational Awareness

- Tailor your serve selection to the match situation. For instance, at critical points or when facing break points, you might opt for a high-percentage serve rather than risking a more aggressive but less reliable serve. Understanding the ebb and flow of a match can inform when to take risks or play conservatively.

Reading the Opponent's Position

An integral part of serving strategy is the ability to read and react to the opponent's position and anticipated movements. Effective servers use this information to make real-time decisions about where to place their serves, thereby maximizing their chances of winning the point outright or gaining a strategic advantage in the ensuing rally. This skill combines observation, prediction, and adaptability, making it a critical aspect of high-level tennis.

Observation

- **Pre-Serve Position:** Before initiating the serve, take a moment to observe your opponent's stance and position. Look for cues such as their distance from the baseline, the side they are favoring, and their grip. This can indicate their comfort zone and potential weaknesses.
- **Return Patterns:** Throughout the match, note your opponent's return patterns on different serves. Some players might struggle with wide serves, while others may be less effective against body serves. Identifying these patterns can inform your serving strategy.

Prediction

- **Anticipating Movement:** Based on your observations, try to predict your opponent's movements. Players often make subtle adjustments before the serve is hit, telegraphing their expectations. For example, if an opponent shifts slightly to cover a wide serve, it might open an opportunity to serve down the T.
- **Tactical Awareness:** Consider the score and the match context. Players might change their return position based on the situation, becoming more aggressive or conservative. Use this information to adjust your serve placement, exploiting their tactical shifts.

Adaptability

- **Adjusting Serve Placement:** Be prepared to adjust your serve placement based on your observations and predictions. Flexibility in your serving approach can keep your opponent off-balance, making it harder for them to mount an effective return game.
- **Varying Serve Types:** Along with placement, vary the types of serves (flat, slice, and kick) to test your opponent's adaptability and expose any weaknesses in their return game.

Fixing Common Serving Mistakes

Even experienced players can fall into patterns that result in common serving mistakes. Identifying and correcting these mistakes is crucial for maintaining a high-quality serve. Here are strategies to address and rectify some of the most frequent serving errors:

Inconsistent Ball Toss

- **Problem:** An inconsistent toss can lead to a wide array of serving errors, making it difficult to develop a reliable and effective serve.
- **Solution:** Focus on the consistency of your ball toss by practicing the toss separately from your serve. Use your fingertips to release the ball, and aim to have it land in the same spot each time. Simplifying your motion can also reduce variables that lead to inconsistency.

Poor Footwork and Stance

- **Problem:** Incorrect footwork and stance can affect the power and accuracy of your serve, leading to balance issues and reduced effectiveness.
- **Solution:** Ensure your stance is balanced and aligned properly with your target. Practice the correct footwork separately, focusing on a smooth transition from the starting position to the point of impact. Incorporating dynamic balance exercises into your training can also help improve stability.

Rushing the Serve

- **Problem:** Rushing through the serve sequence can lead to timing issues and decreased serve quality.
- **Solution:** Develop and adhere to a consistent pre-serve routine that includes a moment of focus before initiating your serve. This routine can help pace your serve, ensuring that each phase of the serve is executed with intention.

Overreliance on Arm Strength

- **Problem:** Relying too much on arm strength rather than using the whole body can limit serve power and lead to an increased risk of injury.
- **Solution:** Focus on engaging your entire body in the serve, especially the legs and core, to generate power from the ground up. Practice drills that emphasize the kinetic chain involved in serving, from leg drive to hip rotation to arm extension.

Hitting Too Hard

- **Problem:** Attempting to hit the serve too hard can compromise control and lead to more faults.
- **Solution:** Concentrate on hitting the serve with optimal speed for the situation, balancing power with precision. Use practice sessions to find a comfortable power level that allows you to maintain control and consistency.

Neglecting Serve Variation

- **Problem:** A lack of serve variation can make your serve predictable and easier for opponents to return.
- **Solution:** Incorporate a mix of serve speeds, spins, and placements into your practice routines. Regularly changing up your serve during matches can keep opponents guessing and create more opportunities for winning points.

Insufficient Practice

- **Problem:** Without regular and focused serve practice, it's challenging to address weaknesses and improve serve performance.
- **Solution:** Dedicate a portion of your practice sessions exclusively to serving, covering various serve types and scenarios. Recording your serve and reviewing the footage can provide insights into areas for improvement.

Addressing these common serving mistakes involves a combination of technical adjustments, mental focus, and consistent practice. By recognizing and correcting these errors, players can enhance the effectiveness of their serve, turning it into a reliable weapon in their tennis arsenal.

Practice Drills for a Powerful Serve

Developing a powerful serve requires consistent practice, focusing on technique, timing, and body mechanics. Here are several drills designed to enhance the power of your serve, each targeting different aspects of the serve's execution.

The Racket Head Speed Drill

- **Objective:** Increase racket head speed, which is crucial for generating power.
- **How to Do It:** Practice serving with only your arm and racket, eliminating the leg drive and toss. Focus on snapping your wrist and forearm through the ball. This isolates the upper-body mechanics and improves racket head speed. Perform this drill with a moderate number of repetitions to avoid arm fatigue.

The Toss and Freeze Drill

- **Objective:** Improve consistency and placement of the ball toss, a key factor in power generation.
- **How to Do It:** Perform your normal serve motion but freeze at the point where you would normally hit the ball. The goal is to ensure that the ball toss is in the ideal spot for a powerful serve every time. If the toss is inconsistent, adjust until you find a reliable placement.

The Leg Drive Drill

- **Objective:** Enhance the contribution of leg power to the serve.
- **How to Do It:** Start your serve with a deep knee bend, emphasizing the explosive push-off from the ground as you move into the serve. Practice serves, focusing on using this leg drive to generate upward and forward momentum. This drill helps integrate leg strength into the serving motion for added power.

The Progressive Power Drill

- **Objective:** Gradually increase serve power while maintaining control and placement.
- **How to Do It:** Begin by serving at 50% power, focusing on technique and ball placement. With each subsequent serve, incrementally increase the power while trying to maintain accuracy. This gradual approach helps you find the balance between power and control.

The Serving Targets Drill

- **Objective:** Develop power with purpose by aiming for specific targets in the service boxes.
- **How to Do It:** Place targets (such as cones or towels) in various parts of the service box to represent different strategic serves (wide, body, and down the line). Practice serving with full power aiming at these targets. This drill not only improves power but also the precision and tactical application of the serve.

The Shadow Serving Drill

- **Objective:** Refine the serving motion and improve muscle memory without the ball.
- **How to Do It:** Perform your serve in slow motion, focusing on each phase of the motion, from the initial stance to the follow-through. This drill allows you to focus on form and fluidity, which are essential for a powerful serve.

Incorporating these drills into your practice sessions will not only increase the power of your serve but also enhance your overall serving technique. Regular, focused practice is key to making lasting improvements. Remember, a powerful serve is not just about brute force; it's about the efficient and effective use of your entire body to generate maximum impact.

VOLLEY FUNDAMENTALS

The volley, executed before the ball bounces, is a pivotal shot in tennis, vital for dominating the net and exerting pressure on opponents. Its mastery is essential for players aiming to enhance their net game. This section delves into the core aspects of volleying, including the forehand volley, backhand volley, and half volley, alongside stance, preparation, and effective drills.

Stance and Preparation

- **The Ready Position**: Adopt a balanced stance, with feet shoulder-width apart and knees slightly bent. This ensures agility and readiness to move in any direction. The weight should be on the balls of your feet for quick responses.
- **Grip**: The continental grip is ideal for both forehand and backhand volleys, facilitating a seamless transition between shots without the need to adjust your grip.
- **Racket Position**: Keep the racket in front of you, slightly above net level, with the face angled forward. This prepares you to intercept the ball early and direct it with precision.

Forehand Volley

- **Position and Movement:** For the forehand volley, lead with the foot opposite your racket hand (left foot for right-handers) as you step into the shot. This ensures balance and adds momentum to the volley.
- **Contact Point:** Hit the ball in front of your body, using a firm wrist to guide the racket head through the point of contact. The swing should be compact, with minimal backswing.
- **Follow-Through:** The follow-through on a forehand volley should be short and directed toward your intended target, emphasizing control over power.

Backhand Volley

- **Position and Movement:** Similar to the forehand, use the foot opposite the racket hand to step into the volley but ensure your shoulders are square to the net for stability and power.
- **Contact Point:** The backhand volley should also be struck out in front of the body. For two-handed players, it's essential to maintain a firm lead hand to guide the shot.
- **Follow-Through:** Keep the follow-through concise and in line with the shot's trajectory. The backhand volley typically requires a firmer wrist than the forehand to maintain control.

Half Volley

- **Definition:** The half volley is a challenging shot played immediately after the ball bounces, requiring precise timing and technique. It's often used when a player cannot reach the ball in the air but still wishes to maintain an aggressive position near the net.
- **Technique:** Bend your knees more deeply than for a standard volley to get closer to the bounce. The racket should meet the ball just as it begins its ascent, with a slight forward push to lift the ball over the net.
- **Follow-Through:** The follow-through on a half volley is minimal, similar to a standard volley, focusing on directing the ball and maintaining control.

Common Mistakes and How to Correct Them

- **Overswinging:** Minimize your backswing to maintain control over the volley.
- **Late Preparation:** Keep your racket prepared and anticipate the shot to improve reaction time.
- **Poor Footwork:** Use dynamic footwork to position yourself optimally for volleys, stepping into the shot for added stability and power.

Drills to Improve Your Volleys

- **Rapid-Fire Volleys:** Partner up and exchange a series of quick volleys to enhance reaction time and precision.
- **Target Practice:** Place targets in various areas of the court to improve accuracy and placement.
- **Solo Wall Practice:** Use a wall to practice forehand, backhand, and half volleys, focusing on maintaining proper form and technique.

Mastering the volley requires understanding these fundamentals and regularly practicing to hone your skills. By focusing on the proper stance, preparation, and execution of forehand, backhand, and half volleys, you'll significantly improve your net game and overall performance on the court.

OVERHEAD SMASH FUNDAMENTALS

Adding to the essential techniques of forehand and backhand volleys, as well as the nuanced half volley, mastering the overhead smash is pivotal for dominating at the net. The overhead smash is a powerful shot used to finish points when the ball is high in the air, combining elements of serve mechanics with volley positioning. This section extends our exploration into the technique and strategy behind executing an effective overhead smash.

Overhead Smash

Positioning and Footwork

- **Preparation:** As soon as you anticipate a lob from your opponent, turn sideways to the net with your non-racket shoulder pointing toward the incoming ball. Use quick, shuffle steps to position yourself under the ball, keeping it slightly in front and to your dominant side.
- **Split Step:** Perform a split step as the ball reaches its peak. This readies you for a dynamic leap and powerful swing.

Grip and Swing

- **Grip:** The continental grip is ideal for overhead smashes, providing the right balance between power and control.
- **Swing Path:** Mimic the motion of your serve. Draw the racket back in a trophy pose, with the racket head pointing upward and the elbow bent. Uncoil your body upward and forward as you swing, making contact with the ball at the highest point possible.

Contact Point and Follow-Through

- **Contact Point:** Aim to hit the ball at its highest point where you can comfortably reach it, ideally in front of your body. This maximizes power and control, directing the ball downward into the opponent's court.
- **Follow-Through:** Follow through with your swing in the direction you intend the ball to go, allowing your racket

to naturally finish over your opposite shoulder. Ensure your body weight transfers from the back foot to the front foot through the shot, enhancing the smash's power.

Common Mistakes and How to Correct Them

- **Poor Positioning:** Not getting under the ball can lead to weak or misdirected smashes.
- *Correction*: Use quick footwork to adjust your position, keeping your eyes on the ball to judge its trajectory accurately.
- **Inadequate Power:** Failing to generate enough power can turn a smash into a setup for your opponent.
- *Correction*: Ensure you're using your whole body to generate power, from your legs through your torso and into your arm swing.
- **Timing Issues:** Hitting the ball too late or too early can compromise the effectiveness of your smash.
- *Correction*: Practice timing your swing so you're hitting the ball at the optimal point. Use drills that simulate lobs to improve your reaction and timing.

Drills to Improve Your Overhead Smash

- **Lob and Smash Drill:** Have a partner or coach feed you lobs of varying height and depth, practicing your positioning, footwork, and smash execution. Aim for consistency and power in your smashes.
- **Solo Shadow Swing:** Without the ball, practice the motion of the overhead smash, focusing on your footwork, trophy pose, and swing path. This helps muscle memory and improves technique.

- **Serve and Smash Combination:** Practice transitioning from a serve to an overhead smash. This drill helps improve footwork, positioning, and the seamless execution of smashes following a serve motion.

Mastering the overhead smash adds a potent weapon to your arsenal, especially for net play. By focusing on proper positioning, grip, and execution, and through consistent practice, you'll become more confident in putting away high balls, thereby enhancing your overall game and putting pressure on opponents.

CASE STUDY: PETE SAMPRAS – MASTER OF SERVES, VOLLEYS, AND OVERHEADS

Pete Sampras, an American tennis player, is often celebrated as one of the greatest players in the history of tennis, particularly noted for his mastery over serves, volleys, and overhead smashes. His playing style, which seamlessly blended power, precision, and finesse, not only dominated men's tennis during the 1990s but also left a lasting impact on the sport. This case study delves into how Sampras's skill set in these areas defined his career and influenced generations of players.

Dominance Through Serve

- **The "Slam Dunk" Serve:** Sampras's serve was a weapon of precision and power. He possessed one of the most formidable second serves in the game, which often acted as an offensive tool rather than merely starting the point. His ability to hit aces under pressure made breaking his serve an arduous task for opponents.
- **Adaptability:** What set Sampras apart was his adaptability in serving. He could effortlessly switch between flat, slice, and kick serves depending on the situation, making him

unpredictable and difficult to read. This versatility was crucial in matches against the top returners of his era.

Volleys – An Art Perfected

- **Net Mastery:** Sampras was renowned for his volleying skills, which are a testament to his exceptional hand-eye coordination and anticipation. His approach to the net was aggressive yet calculated, often following a powerful serve or a well-placed groundstroke, forcing opponents into difficult positions.
- **Technique and Touch:** Beyond power, Sampras's volleys exhibited a delicate touch, allowing him to place shots with precision. His ability to execute both backhand and forehand volleys with equal finesse made him a formidable opponent at the net.

Overhead Smashes – Sealing Points With Authority

- **Athleticism and Timing:** Sampras's overhead smashes were a display of his athletic prowess. He could track down lobs with ease, positioning himself perfectly to unleash a smash. His timing and ability to judge the ball's trajectory stood out, often turning defensive positions into offensive opportunities.
- **Power and Placement:** His smashes were not just powerful but also well-placed, often leaving opponents with no chance of retrieval. Sampras used his overheads not just to win points but to send a message of dominance, contributing to the psychological battle on the court.

Legacy and Influence

- **A Complete Player:** Sampras's proficiency in serves, volleys, and overheads made him one of the most complete players of his time. His game was built on the foundation of these shots, allowing him to dominate on all surfaces.
- **Influence on Future Generations:** The success and style of Sampras have influenced countless players, highlighting the importance of a strong serve-and-volley game in an era increasingly dominated by baseline play. Players like Roger Federer have cited Sampras as an inspiration, adopting elements of his game into their own.

Pete Sampras's career, marked by 14 Grand Slam titles and numerous other accolades, showcases the effectiveness of mastering serves, volleys, and overheads. Sampras retired in 2002 but left behind a legacy that continues to influence the sport. His mastery of serves, volleys, and overheads remains a high benchmark for players aiming to excel in these critical aspects of the game. Pete Sampras's career exemplifies how a well-rounded game, built on the foundation of exceptional serving and net play, can lead to dominance in the highly competitive world of professional tennis.

Now that you have a basic understanding of the different strokes, it's time to practice and fine-tune your game. Equipped with the fundamental knowledge, you're poised to bring theory to life. In Chapter 4, "Training and Practice Routines," we embark on the practical journey of tennis. This next chapter introduces different ways to practice and proper coaching to elevate you from a casual player to a formidable competitor. It's time to lace up, grip your racket tightly, and confidently step onto the court. The game of tennis awaits your participation and potential triumphs.

TRAINING AND PRACTICE ROUTINES

I magine stepping onto the court for the first time, the fresh scent of tennis balls mixing with the anticipation in the air. This is the moment where the journey truly begins, transforming from a beginner holding a racket to a player ready for their first match. It's a path filled with challenges and triumphs, each practice session laying another stone on the road to competence. This transformative journey isn't just about learning to hit the ball; it's about embracing the discipline and dedication required to play the game. It's about turning the nervous energy of the first serve into the exhilarating rush of your first win.

As we embark on Chapter 4, "Training and Practice Routines," we delve into the practice preparations that turn a novice into a player, ready to face the challenges of the court with confidence and skill. Your first match marks not the end but the beginning of an ongoing journey of growth and discovery in tennis.

SOLO PRACTICE SESSIONS

Solo Drills and Exercises

While tennis is inherently a social sport involving either a partner or an opponent, solo drills and exercises are invaluable for focusing on specific areas of improvement without the variability of another player. Here's how to effectively utilize technology and equipment in your solo training regimen:

Ball Machines

- **Consistent Repetition:** Ball machines offer a consistent and reliable way to practice specific shots or patterns without needing a partner. Adjust the speed, spin, and direction to work on various aspects of your game, from groundstrokes to volleys.
- **Endurance and Movement Drills:** Set up the ball machine to simulate point play conditions, challenging your movement and endurance as you respond to a sequence of shots.

Video Analysis Tools

- **Technique Breakdown:** Use video recording equipment to capture your practice sessions and matches. Analyzing these videos can help identify technical flaws in your strokes, footwork, and positioning that might not be apparent in real-time.
- **Performance Tracking:** Advanced software can provide detailed analytics, such as ball speed, spin rate, and shot placement, allowing for a quantitative assessment of your game.

Online Training Platforms

- **Remote Coaching:** Utilize online platforms that offer virtual coaching sessions, where you can receive personalized feedback and instruction from coaches anywhere in the world.
- **Instructional Content:** Access a wealth of instructional videos and tutorials that cover every aspect of tennis, from technique to strategy and mental training.

Wearable Fitness Trackers

- **Physical Conditioning Monitoring:** Wearable devices can track your heart rate, distance covered, and calories burned during practice sessions, providing valuable data on your physical exertion and conditioning levels.
- **Recovery Analysis:** Some trackers also monitor sleep patterns and recovery metrics, helping you optimize rest periods and prevent overtraining.

Racket Sensors

- **Swing Analysis:** Attachable sensors can analyze your racket speed, ball impact point, and swing patterns, offering insights into your hitting mechanics. This data can help refine your strokes for greater efficiency and power.
- **Progress Tracking:** By collecting data over time, racket sensors allow you to track improvements in your game, setting and achieving quantifiable targets for your strokes.

Smart Courts and Simulation Technology

- **Detailed Analytics:** Smart courts equipped with cameras and sensors provide comprehensive analytics on shot placement, player movement, and tactical patterns, offering a holistic view of performance.
- **Virtual Reality:** Simulation technology and virtual reality can recreate match scenarios, allowing players to practice strategy and decision-making in a controlled environment.

Maximizing the Benefits

- **Selective Integration:** Choose technology and equipment that specifically address your training needs and goals. Avoid overwhelming yourself with too much data or too many gadgets.
- **Combine With Traditional Training:** Ensure that technology complements rather than replaces fundamental on-court practice and physical conditioning. The human element of coaching and partner feedback remains irreplaceable.

By thoughtfully incorporating technology and specialized equipment into your training, you can unlock new dimensions of performance analysis and improvement. These tools not only provide objective data and feedback but also introduce innovative ways to engage with and enjoy the process of developing your tennis game.

Learning From the Pros

Having role models in tennis serves as a significant source of inspiration, motivation, and guidance for players at all levels. Role models, whether they are past legends or current professionals, provide a blueprint for success, demonstrating the heights achievable through dedication, skill, and mental fortitude. Through analyzing professional matches, players at all levels can gain insights into advanced techniques, strategies, and mental approaches that can be adapted to their own games. Here are several ways to analyze professional matches:

Technical Observations

- **Stroke Mechanics:** Pay close attention to the pros' stroke production, including their footwork, racket preparation, and follow-through. Note how they adjust their technique based on different situations, such as baseline rallies versus net play.
- **Serve and Return:** Analyze serve mechanics, placement, and variety, as well as return positioning and strategies. Understanding how professionals adapt these critical aspects of their game can offer valuable lessons in effectiveness and adaptability.

Tactical Insights

- **Point Construction:** Observe how professionals construct points, using a combination of shots to outmaneuver their opponents. Note their use of depth, angles, and spin to control rallies and create openings.
- **Adaptation to Opponents:** Focus on how players adjust their tactics based on their opponent's strengths and weaknesses. This can provide lessons in flexibility and strategic thinking that are applicable at any level of play.

Mental Approach

- **Pressure Situations:** Pay special attention to how professionals handle high-pressure situations, such as break points or tiebreaks. Observe their body language, routines, and shot selection to glean insights into their mental resilience and focus.
- **Emotional Management:** Notice how players manage their emotions after winning or losing points. Learning from how the pros regain composure or maintain momentum can enhance your emotional control on the court.

Physical Conditioning and Recovery

- **Athleticism and Endurance:** Note the physicality and endurance displayed by professionals during long matches. Observing their movement patterns and recovery strategies can emphasize the importance of physical conditioning in your own training regimen.
- **In-Match Recovery:** Observe how players utilize changeovers and between-point moments for physical and mental recovery. These practices can be incorporated into your routine to improve in-match endurance and focus.

Match Analysis Techniques

- **Selective Focus:** Instead of watching a match passively, choose a specific aspect to focus on, such as a player's backhand or their decision-making on break points. This targeted approach can provide deeper insights into particular skills or strategies.

- **Use of Technology:** Take advantage of slow-motion replays and statistical analysis available during professional broadcasts to understand the nuances of match play. Technology can highlight aspects of the game that might not be apparent at full speed.
- **Note-Taking and Reflection:** Keep a notebook during match analysis to jot down observations, questions, and potential areas of improvement for your own game. Reflecting on these notes can help translate observations into actionable insights.

By analyzing professional matches, players can uncover a wealth of knowledge that can inspire and inform their own path to improvement. This practice encourages a critical eye toward the game, fostering a deeper understanding of tennis's technical, tactical, and mental dimensions.

PRACTICE PARTNERS

Practice partners are an essential aspect of tennis training, offering opportunities for live ball drills, match play simulations, and immediate feedback. This dynamic environment of practicing with peers replicates match conditions more closely than solo practice, challenging your reactions, decision-making, and adaptability. Here's how to maximize the benefits of practicing with a partner:

Live Ball Drills

- **Rally Consistency:** Engage in baseline rallies, aiming for consistency and depth. Set goals such as hitting a certain number of shots in a row without errors.

- **Directional Control:** Practice controlling the direction of your shots with your partner or coach, alternating between cross-court and down-the-line shots to improve accuracy and shot placement.

Match Play and Point Construction

- **Situational Points:** Simulate specific match situations (e.g., break points, deuce games) to practice strategic responses and mental resilience under pressure.
- **Serve and Return Games:** Focus on the serve and return by playing games that start with the serve. This helps improve first-serve percentage, second-serve reliability, and return aggressiveness.

Tactical Training

- **Pattern Play:** Work on developing point patterns that play to your strengths. For example, practice a serve out wide, followed by a forehand into the open court.
- **Strategy Implementation:** Use practice sessions to experiment with and refine match strategies, such as adjusting to your partner's playing style or working on neutralizing specific types of shots.

Feedback and Correction

- **Immediate Feedback:** An experienced partner can provide instant feedback on technique, strategy, and mental approach, offering insights that are difficult to self-diagnose.
- **Technical Adjustments:** Use this feedback to make immediate corrections, with your coach or partner

observing and guiding adjustments to your strokes, footwork, or positioning.

Competitive Scenarios

- **Set Play:** Playing full sets or practice matches with a partner helps simulate the physical and mental demands of competitive play, including dealing with momentum shifts and managing game strategies.

Doubles Practice

- If doubles play is part of your competitive focus, practicing with a partner becomes even more critical. Work on communication, positioning, and specific doubles tactics, such as poaching and effective net play.

Physical Conditioning

- Incorporate movement and conditioning drills that require two people, such as medicine ball exercises, synchronized agility drills, or competitive sprint challenges, to add variety and fun to physical training.

Maximizing Practice Efficiency

- **Plan Ahead:** Before the session, discuss your goals and focus areas with your partner to ensure the practice is structured and productive.
- **Regular Review:** After practice sessions, take time to review what worked well and what needs improvement and plan adjustments for future practices.

Practicing with a partner not only enhances technical skills and strategic understanding but also develops the competitive edge required for match play. By incorporating a variety of drills, match simulations, and feedback mechanisms into these sessions, players can significantly improve their performance and readiness for competition.

TENNIS CAMPS AND CLINICS

Tennis camps and clinics offer unique environments for intensive learning and development, providing players of all levels with the opportunity to refine their skills, learn new strategies, and immerse themselves in a focused tennis setting. These programs are designed not only to improve technical and tactical aspects of the game but also to foster personal growth, resilience, and a deeper understanding of tennis. Here are some of the key benefits of participating in tennis camps and clinics:

Comprehensive Skill Development

- **Focused Training:** Camps and clinics often provide comprehensive training sessions that cover all aspects of the game, from stroke mechanics and footwork to strategy and mental toughness. This holistic approach ensures balanced skill development.
- **High-Quality Coaching:** Participants have access to experienced and certified coaches who can offer personalized feedback and insights, helping players identify and work on specific areas of improvement.

Intensive Practice Environment

- **Immersive Experience:** The immersive nature of camps and clinics allows players to dedicate significant time and focus to tennis, accelerating learning and improvement through intensive practice and instruction.
- **Structured Schedule:** The structured and disciplined schedule of these programs promotes a professional approach to training, encouraging players to adopt similar routines in their regular practice.

Exposure to Diverse Playing Styles

- **Varied Opponents:** Tennis camps and clinics attract players from different regions and backgrounds, exposing participants to a variety of playing styles and strategies. This diversity enhances adaptability and tactical flexibility.
- **Match Play:** Many programs include match play sessions or mini-tournaments, providing valuable competitive experience and the opportunity to apply newly learned skills and strategies in a match setting.

Mental and Physical Conditioning

- **Mental Skills Workshops:** Some camps and clinics offer workshops on mental toughness, concentration, and emotional control, equipping players with strategies to enhance their mental game.
- **Physical Fitness:** Alongside technical training, physical conditioning sessions improve overall fitness, strength, and agility, which are crucial for performance and injury prevention.

Cost-Effectiveness

- Attending tennis camps and clinics offers the advantage of receiving high-quality coaching and structured practice sessions at a fraction of the cost of one-on-one coaching, providing an affordable way to improve your game and learn from experienced instructors alongside peers.

Tennis camps and clinics represent valuable opportunities for players to significantly advance their game, immerse themselves in a supportive and challenging learning environment, and foster connections within the tennis community. By participating in these programs, players can accelerate their development, gain new perspectives on their game, and take meaningful steps toward achieving their tennis goals.

ONE-ON-ONE COACHING

In the pursuit of tennis excellence, one-on-one coaching is indispensable for development. Coaches provide objective insights into a player's performance, highlighting strengths to be leveraged and areas needing improvement. This section explores the crucial role of coaching in facilitating continuous growth and the ways in which players can actively seek and utilize feedback to enhance their game.

Finding the Right Coach

Identifying and collaborating with the right coach is pivotal in a tennis player's journey toward improvement and mastery. A coach not only imparts technical skills and tactical knowledge but also plays a critical role in developing a player's mental game, work ethic, and approach to the sport. Here are strategies to ensure you find a coach who aligns with your goals, personality, and aspirations:

Define Your Goals and Needs

- **Clarity of Objectives:** Before starting your search, be clear about what you want to achieve in tennis and what areas of your game need the most attention. This clarity will help you find a coach who specializes in those areas.
- **Personal Compatibility:** Consider your learning style and personality traits. Finding a coach whose teaching approach and personality complement yours can significantly enhance the effectiveness of the coaching relationship.

Research and Recommendations

- **Seek Recommendations:** Ask fellow players, tennis clubs, or local associations for recommendations. Personal endorsements can provide valuable insights into a coach's effectiveness, style, and rapport with players.
- **Check Credentials and Experience:** Look for coaches with recognized certifications, relevant experience, and a track record of developing players with similar goals to yours. Experience in playing at a high level can also be beneficial, though not strictly necessary.

Evaluate Coaching Philosophy

- **Philosophy and Approach:** Inquire about the coach's philosophy and approach to training, development, and competition. Ensure their philosophy aligns with your goals and values as a player.

- **Commitment to Continuous Learning:** Choose a coach who demonstrates a commitment to their own continuous learning and adaptation. This quality is crucial for staying updated with the latest techniques, strategies, and mental training methods.

Communication and Feedback Style

- **Open Lines of Communication:** A coach should offer clear, honest, and constructive feedback in a manner that resonates with you. Effective communication is key to understanding and implementing feedback for improvement.
- **Feedback Frequency:** Discuss how often you'll receive feedback and through what means (e.g., verbal feedback during sessions, written reports, video analysis). Regular, structured feedback is essential for tracking progress and making adjustments.

Trial Sessions

- **Arrange Trial Sessions:** Before making a commitment, arrange a few trial sessions with potential coaches. This firsthand experience will give you insights into their coaching style, interaction, and the value they could bring to your development.
- **Assess Compatibility:** Use trial sessions to assess compatibility, communication, and whether the coach's insights and instructions lead to noticeable improvements, even in a short period.

Consider Logistics and Commitment

- **Availability and Location:** Ensure the coach's availability aligns with your schedule and that their location is feasible for regular sessions. Consider the commitment required in terms of time, travel, and finances.
- **Long-Term Potential:** Look for a coach with whom you can envision building a long-term relationship. Continuous improvement in tennis requires time, and having a stable coaching relationship can provide a solid foundation for growth.

Finding the right coach is a critical decision in a tennis player's career. The ideal coach not only improves your game technically and tactically but also supports your personal growth, challenges you to exceed your limits, and inspires you to pursue excellence with passion and dedication.

CASE STUDY: JUSTINE HENIN – A LEGACY OF CONTINUOUS IMPROVEMENT AND ADAPTATION

Justine Henin, the Belgian tennis prodigy, etched her name into the annals of tennis history with a career that exemplified sheer talent, relentless pursuit of excellence, and an unwavering commitment to continuous improvement and adaptation. Standing at 5'5" (1.67m), Henin's stature belied the enormity of her presence on the court, challenging and often overcoming taller and stronger opponents with her skill, strategy, and indomitable spirit. This case study explores Henin's illustrious career, her dedication to refining her game, and her ability to adapt to the evolving landscape of women's tennis.

Achievements and Highlights

Henin's career is studded with notable achievements, including seven Grand Slam titles, including four at the French Open, showcasing her mastery on clay. Her versatility across surfaces was evident in her wins at the Australian Open (2004) and the US Open (2003, 2007). Henin also achieved the coveted World No. 1 ranking, holding it for a total of 117 weeks.

Her 2007 season was particularly remarkable, as she won 10 titles, including two Grand Slams, and finished the year as the world No. 1, demonstrating her dominance in the sport.

Continuous Improvement and Adaptation

- **Evolving Game Style**: Henin's commitment to improvement saw her continually refine her game. Early in her career, she was known for her baseline play and stunning backhand. However, recognizing the need to diversify her game, Henin developed a formidable net game, making her one of the best volleyers in women's tennis. This addition made her unpredictable and more challenging to defeat.
- **Physical and Mental Conditioning**: Henin's physical preparation and mental fortitude were key components of her training regime. She worked tirelessly to improve her strength and endurance, enabling her to compete in grueling matches against physically stronger opponents. Mentally, Henin focused on cultivating resilience, often turning the tide in matches through sheer willpower and strategic intelligence.
- **Adaptation to Competition and Injury**: Henin's career was not without challenges, facing stiff competition from

contemporaries like Serena Williams and battling injuries that sidelined her at crucial moments. Each time, Henin adapted her approach, whether it meant altering her training to prevent injuries or modifying her tactics to counter the power-based game of her rivals.

Legacy

Henin's legacy is characterized by her exquisite technique, particularly her one-handed backhand, her strategic acumen, and her unyielding pursuit of excellence. She remains an inspiration for players who emphasize skill, strategy, and adaptability over sheer power. Henin's career success, marked by her continuous improvement and adaptation, ensures her place among the legends of tennis, celebrated for changing the dynamics of the game and demonstrating that grace, precision, and mental strength are just as potent as power and athleticism.

Now that you've learned the different ways to practice and find coaching, it's time to discuss point play strategy. In

With your game finely tuned through countless practice sessions, it's time to expand your focus to the broader dynamics of match play. Practice settings are just the beginning; how you play the points in match conditions can define your style, strategy, and success on the court. From constructing rallies with the intention to mastering the art of point closure, every stroke you play contributes to the narrative of the match.

As we transition to Chapter 5, "Playing the Points," we'll delve into strategies for rally construction, shot selection, and adapting to the ever-changing conditions of a match. This chapter will equip you with the insights and tactics needed to navigate points effectively, allowing you to capitalize on your serve and maintain control of the game. Let's explore the comprehensive skills that complete your tennis repertoire, ensuring you're prepared for every opportunity to claim the point.

PLAYING THE POINTS

Picture yourself in a tiebreak—a thrilling, point-by-point duel under the glaring lights of a grand slam final, with the score locked in a deadlock, and each player just points away from victory. It begins with a carefully placed serve, followed by a series of blistering groundstrokes, daring volleys, and strategic lobs, each shot a testament to the players' mastery and mental toughness. Rallies ebb and flow like tides, with momentum shifting unpredictably between the competitors. Every point is a battle, and the margin for error is razor-thin. The tiebreak stands as the ultimate test of nerve, skill, and strategy.

As we embark on Chapter 5, "Playing the Points," let's dive into the strategies and subtleties that turn each point into an opportunity, each shot into a statement, and every game into a step toward victory. Through this exploration, we'll uncover the art and science behind playing the points, transforming each rally into a narrative of resilience, innovation, and mastery.

RALLYING FOR SUCCESS

Building Consistency in Your Strokes

In the dynamic landscape of a tennis match, the ability to rally effectively serves as the backbone of success. Central to this is building consistency in your strokes, ensuring that you can not only initiate but also sustain exchanges until an opportunity to win the point presents itself. Consistency is about reliability and precision, minimizing unforced errors while applying pressure on your opponent. Here are key strategies to enhance the consistency of your strokes:

Master the Fundamentals

- Focus on perfecting the basic techniques of each stroke, from grip to follow-through. Consistent strokes are built on a foundation of sound mechanics. Regularly review and refine your technique, paying attention to footwork, racket head speed, and point of contact.

Practice With Purpose

- Engage in drills designed to improve stroke consistency. This can include hitting balls from a basket to focus on specific technical aspects or rallying from the baseline to simulate match conditions. Incorporate targets into your practice to refine accuracy and control.

Develop a Solid Rally Tempo

- Establish a comfortable rally tempo that allows you to hit effective shots without overexerting yourself. This involves selecting appropriate shot speeds and spins that you can sustain over long rallies. Practicing at this tempo helps build muscle memory and confidence in your strokes.

Implement Mental Routines

- Consistency is not just physical but also mental. Develop pre-point routines that help you focus and stay present during rallies. This can include deep breathing, positive self-talk, or visualizing successful shots. Mental routines can keep you calm and collected, allowing you to execute with precision under pressure.

Improve Your Fitness

- Physical conditioning plays a significant role in stroke consistency. Work on your overall fitness, with a focus on stamina, strength, and agility. A well-conditioned body can maintain high levels of performance throughout matches, reducing the risk of fatigue-related errors.

Manage Your Shot Selection

- Wise shot selection is crucial for maintaining rally consistency. Avoid high-risk shots when unnecessary, and opt for strategic placement over sheer power. Understanding when to change pace or spin, when to attack, and when to play defensively can keep you in points longer and force errors from your opponent.

Adjust to Playing Conditions

- Be adaptable to different court surfaces, weather conditions, and opponents. Each factor can affect the behavior of your shots and the overall dynamics of rallies. Learning to adjust your stroke mechanics and strategies accordingly can enhance your consistency across diverse playing scenarios.

Analyze and Learn

- Regularly analyze your performance, identifying areas of strength and those requiring improvement. This can be done through video analysis, feedback from coaches, or self-reflection. Learning from both successes and mistakes allows for continual growth in stroke consistency.

Building consistency in your strokes is a multifaceted process that combines technical proficiency, strategic awareness, physical conditioning, and mental fortitude. By dedicating time to developing these aspects, you can create a reliable and effective rallying game, capable of weathering the challenges posed by different opponents and conditions and, ultimately, leading to greater success on the court.

Controlling the Pace of the Game

Controlling the pace of the game is a critical strategy in tennis that involves dictating the speed and rhythm of play to your advantage. By managing the pace, you can exert pressure on your opponent, force them into uncomfortable situations, and conserve your own energy for crucial moments. Here's how to effectively control the pace of the game through rallying:

Strategic Shot Selection

- Choosing the right shot at the right time is pivotal to pace control. Use deep, powerful groundstrokes to push your opponent back and slow down the game, or employ short angles and drop shots to speed it up and disrupt their rhythm. Mixing up your shots keeps your opponent guessing and prevents them from settling into a comfortable pace.

Varying Spin and Speed

- Incorporate a variety of spins and speeds into your shots. Topspin shots with high arcs give you more time to recover and set up for the next shot, effectively slowing down the point. Flat, hard-hitting shots increase the pace, applying pressure on your opponent to react quickly. Slice shots can be used to change the game's tempo, often forcing slower, lower bounces that disrupt timing.

Serve and Return Tactics

- The serve and return are crucial in establishing the point's pace. A well-placed serve can start the point on your terms, allowing you to control the rally from the outset. Similarly, an aggressive return can immediately put your opponent on the defensive, dictating the pace from the very first shot.

Court Positioning

- Take control of the baseline to dictate the pace, keeping your opponent moving and preventing them from stepping in and taking charge of the rally. Conversely, moving in to take balls early or approaching the net can speed up the point and force quicker exchanges.

Using the Pause

- Employ strategic pauses between points to manage the overall pace of the match. Use the time to gather your thoughts, plan your next move, and disrupt your opponent's momentum. However, be mindful of the rules and maintain sportsmanship regarding pacing.

Physical Conditioning

- Being in top physical condition allows you to endure long rallies and matches, giving you the upper hand in controlling the pace. If you're confident in your fitness, you can push the pace to wear down opponents or choose to extend rallies, knowing you can outlast them.

Mental Resilience

- Staying mentally tough is essential for pace control. Being able to stick to your game plan, even under pressure, allows you to maintain the pace you've set regardless of the score or momentum shifts.

Practice Drills

- **Speed Variation Drills:** Practice hitting balls with different speeds and spins, focusing on transitioning smoothly between them.

- **Rally Length Control:** Play practice points where the goal is to extend rallies to a certain number of shots, emphasizing movement and recovery.
- **Pressure Situation Simulations:** Simulate match scenarios where you must control the pace under pressure, such as serving for the set or breaking serve to stay in the match.

Mastering the art of controlling the pace of the game requires a blend of strategic shot-making, physical preparation, and mental fortitude. By implementing these strategies, you can dictate the flow of the match, keeping opponents within your tactical grasp while playing to your strengths.

Using Angles and Depth to Your Advantage

In tennis, effectively using angles and depth in your shots can significantly enhance your rallying success. These elements introduce complexity and variety into your game, forcing opponents to cover more of the court and often putting them in defensive positions. Mastering the strategic use of angles and depth allows you to control rallies, conserve energy, and create opportunities for winning shots.

Maximizing Angles

- **Creating Wide Angles:** Utilize cross-court shots to create wide angles that stretch your opponent across the court. This not only makes it difficult for them to return the ball but also opens up the court for your next shot. Practice hitting cross-court from both wings, aiming to place the ball close to the sidelines.

- **Short Angles:** Short-angled shots are a potent weapon, especially when executed with a slice or topspin. These shots land near the service line and bounce off sharply, forcing your opponent to move forward and to the side, often pulling them out of position.
- **Net Play and Volleys:** When at the net, angles become even more effective due to your closer court position. A well-placed angled volley can be nearly impossible to return. Focus on soft touch and precision to drop the ball just over the net at wide angles.

Utilizing Depth

- **Deep Shots to the Baseline:** Consistently hitting deep shots to your opponent's baseline pushes them back, limiting their ability to attack and giving you control of the rally. Aim for depth with both your forehand and backhand, practicing driving the ball to land just inside the baseline.
- **Varying Depth:** Mixing deep shots with shorter ones can disrupt your opponent's rhythm and force them to constantly adjust their positioning. This variation can lead to errors or weaker returns that you can capitalize on.

Drills for Practicing Angles and Depth

- **Target Practice:** Place targets or cones in various parts of the court to represent desired angles and depths. Practice hitting these targets from different positions on the court to develop accuracy and control.
- **Cross-Court Rallies:** Engage in cross-court rallying drills with a partner, focusing on creating wide angles. Set goals for consecutive angled shots to build consistency.

- **Depth Control Drills:** Use the service boxes as markers for short shots and the area just inside the baseline for deep shots. Alternate between aiming for these areas to practice controlling the depth of your shots.

Strategic Considerations

- **Opponent Weaknesses:** Tailor your use of angles and depth based on your opponent's movement and stroke weaknesses. For example, if they struggle with mobility, use wide angles to stretch them across the court.
- **Court Surface:** Consider the court surface when using angles and depth. For instance, angled shots can be more effective on clay due to the surface's slower speed and higher bounce, giving you more time to recover and set up for the next shot.

Mastering the strategic use of angles and depth in your shots can transform your rallying game, providing you with tools to outmaneuver and outplay opponents. By incorporating these elements into your practice routine and match play, you'll develop a more dynamic and challenging game that leverages the full dimensions of the tennis court.

Stamina Management During Long Rallies

Long rallies are a test of both technical skill and physical endurance in tennis. Managing your stamina effectively during these exchanges is crucial to maintaining a high level of play throughout a match. Proper stamina management can help you outlast your opponent in grueling points and preserve energy for critical moments. Here are strategies to manage your stamina during long rallies:

Efficient Movement

- **Economy of Motion:** Focus on moving efficiently around the court, using the least amount of energy necessary to get into position for each shot. This means taking direct paths to the ball and utilizing split steps to minimize unnecessary movements.
- **Anticipation:** Improve your ability to anticipate your opponent's shots. Reading cues from their body language and racket position can allow you to start moving before the ball is hit, reducing the need for sudden, energy-intensive sprints.

Controlled Breathing

- **Breath Control:** Incorporate controlled breathing into your play. Deep, rhythmic breathing helps maintain oxygen flow to your muscles, reducing fatigue. Breathe in when preparing for a shot and exhale upon contact to maintain a steady breathing pattern during rallies.
- **Relaxation:** Use breaths between points to relax your body and mind. Reducing tension can help conserve energy and improve focus.

Shot Selection

- **Conservative Shot-Making:** Choose shots that maintain rally pressure without overexerting yourself. High-percentage shots that keep the ball deep and in play can force your opponent to work harder, shifting the physical burden to them.
- **Use of Spin:** Incorporate topspin to maintain depth and control with less physical effort than flat, power-driven

shots. Topspin shots also have a higher margin for error, reducing the risk of exhausting rallies due to unforced errors.

Physical Conditioning

- **Endurance Training:** Regular cardiovascular training improves your overall stamina, enabling you to maintain intensity over longer periods. Incorporate activities like running, cycling, or swimming into your fitness regimen.
- **Strength and Flexibility:** Building muscular strength and flexibility can also aid stamina management. Stronger muscles endure longer, and flexibility can prevent energy-draining muscle tightness.

Tactical Pauses

- **Strategic Use of Time:** Utilize the time between points wisely. Walk slowly back to the baseline, use towel breaks, and take your time setting up for serves to catch your breath and mentally prepare for the next point.
- **Mental Resilience:** Develop mental strategies to stay focused and positive during long rallies. A strong mental game can reduce the perception of fatigue and keep you competitively sharp.

Practice Long Rallies

- **Rally Length Drills:** Practice with drills designed to simulate long rallies. This not only improves your physical endurance but also helps you refine the strategies for energy conservation under rally conditions.
- **Match Simulation:** Play practice sets focusing on extending rally length, which can help acclimate your body

and mind to the demands of long points.

Effective stamina management during long rallies is a combination of physical preparedness, efficient on-court strategies, and mental resilience. By incorporating these approaches into your training and match play, you can enhance your ability to compete vigorously in prolonged exchanges, giving you a critical edge in endurance-centric matches.

STRATEGIES FOR SINGLES

Understanding Court Positioning

Court positioning in singles tennis is a fundamental aspect that can significantly influence the dynamics of a match. Proper positioning allows you to cover the court efficiently, dictate play, and respond effectively to your opponent's shots. It involves strategic movement and awareness, enabling you to anticipate and counter your opponent's strategies while creating opportunities to exploit their weaknesses. Here's how understanding and optimizing court positioning can enhance your singles game:

Baseline Play

- **Offensive Positioning:** Standing just behind the baseline allows you to take control of rallies with groundstrokes, applying pressure on your opponent. From this position, you can hit deep shots to push your opponent back or create angles to move them from side to side.
- **Defensive Positioning:** When under pressure, moving slightly further back from the baseline gives you more time to react to your opponent's shots. This position is beneficial for retrieving powerful shots and extending

rallies, allowing you to reset the point and look for opportunities to regain the offensive.

Approaching the Net

- **Transitioning Forward:** Knowing when to move forward into the court is crucial for successful net play. Approach the net behind strong shots that put your opponent on the defensive, reducing their chances of passing you. Ideal approach shots are deep and to the corners, forcing a weaker return.
- **Volley Positioning:** Once at the net, position yourself to cover the most likely angles of return. This usually means standing in the middle of your opponent's possible passing shots, ready to volley with reach to both sides of the court.

Service and Return

- **Serving Position:** Vary your position on the baseline when serving to change the angles and spins of your serves. This variation can keep your opponent guessing and create more challenging return scenarios for them.
- **Return Position:** Adjust your stance based on your opponent's serving patterns. Standing further back can give you more time to react to powerful serves, while stepping inside the baseline can be effective against weaker serves, allowing you to take control early in the point.

Defending Wide Shots

- **Recovery Position:** After hitting a wide shot, immediately move toward the center of the court to cover your opponent's potential responses. The goal is to position yourself in a way that allows you to reach the next shot with minimal movement, conserving energy, and maintaining strategic positioning.

Practice Drills for Court Positioning

- **Baseline Movement Drill:** Practice hitting from the baseline and immediately moving to recover to a central position. This drill enhances your ability to return to a neutral court position quickly after each shot.
- **Approach and Volley Drill:** Work on transitioning from the baseline to the net, focusing on the timing of your approach and your positioning for volleys. Include shots to various areas of the court to simulate match scenarios.
- **Service Box Targets:** During serve practice, use targets to practice hitting different areas of the service box from various positions on the baseline, developing precision and strategic serving.

Understanding and mastering court positioning in singles tennis allows you to play more strategically, conserve energy, and pressure your opponent effectively. By continuously assessing and adjusting your position relative to the ball, your opponent, and the court, you can enhance your ability to dictate the pace and direction of the match.

Attack and Defense: When to Switch

Mastering the balance between offensive and defensive play is crucial for success in singles tennis. Knowing when to attack and when to defend can significantly influence the outcome of a point, a game, or even an entire match. This strategic decision-making relies on assessing the situation, understanding your strengths and weaknesses, and reading your opponent's play. Here are insights into making the pivotal decision to switch between attack and defense:

Recognizing Opportunities to Attack

- **Weak Returns:** Capitalize on weak or short returns by stepping into the court and hitting an aggressive shot, aiming to either win the point outright or gain a commanding position in the rally.
- **Predictable Patterns:** If you notice a pattern in your opponent's play that leaves them vulnerable (e.g., a tendency to slice backhands defensively), prepare to attack when this pattern emerges.
- **Physical and Mental Advantage:** When you sense your opponent is tired or losing focus, increase your aggression to put additional pressure on them, potentially leading to errors or short balls that you can attack.

Identifying Moments for Defense

- **Powerful Shots From Opponent:** When faced with a powerful shot or a well-placed serve, focus on getting the ball back in play with depth or using a slice to neutralize the pace. Defense in these scenarios is about extending the rally and waiting for a better opportunity to counterattack.
- **Out of Position:** If a shot forces you out of position, prioritize returning the ball in a way that allows you to recover and get back into the point rather than attempting a risky shot.
- **High-Risk Situations:** In crucial points or when leading, it may be wise to adopt a more defensive strategy, reducing unforced errors and forcing your opponent to take risks.

Strategies for Effective Transitioning

- **Counterpunching:** Develop the ability to turn defense into offense by counterpunching. This involves defensive shots that are hit with enough accuracy and pace to put your opponent on the defensive, allowing you to regain control of the rally.
- **Positional Awareness:** Always be aware of your court position and that of your opponent. Good positioning allows you to more easily switch between attack and defense, depending on the situation.
- **Anticipation and Footwork:** Improve your anticipation skills and footwork to quickly adjust your positioning and shot selection. Being able to move effectively across the court is key to transitioning between offensive and defensive play.

Practice Drills

- **Attack/Defense Transition Drill:** Practice points where the goal is to switch from defense to attack within the rally, based on coach or partner cues. This helps develop the ability to recognize and seize opportunities to change the rally's momentum.
- **Positional Play Drill:** Work on hitting shots from various court positions, focusing on shot selection that aligns with offensive or defensive strategies. Include movement drills that simulate recovering from wide or deep shots.

Understanding when to attack and when to defend in singles tennis requires a blend of tactical knowledge, situational awareness, and adaptive play. By honing these skills and making informed decisions about when to switch between attack and defense, you can dictate the pace of the game, exploit your opponent's weaknesses, and enhance your overall effectiveness on the court.

Utilizing the Whole Court

Maximizing the use of the entire tennis court is a strategic approach that can significantly enhance your singles game. By effectively utilizing the whole court, you create more angles, introduce greater variety into your shots, and force your opponent to cover more ground, thereby increasing their chances of making errors or giving you easier balls to attack. Here's how to strategically use the entire court to your advantage:

Creating Angles

- **Shot Placement:** Practice hitting shots that create wide angles, pulling your opponent off the court. This not only makes it harder for them to return the ball but also opens up the court for your next shot. Both forehand and backhand sides can be exploited to generate these angles.
- **Serve and Return:** Use angled serves and returns to immediately put your opponent in a defensive position, setting up the point in your favor from the outset.

Depth Variation

- **Deep Shots:** Consistently hitting deep shots to the baseline pins your opponent back, limiting their ability to attack and giving you control of the rally. Deep shots also increase the likelihood of drawing errors from opponents who struggle with balls at their feet.

- **Short Balls:** Mix in drop shots or short angles to bring your opponent forward, disrupting their rhythm and forcing them to play uncomfortable shots. This contrast between deep and short balls can be particularly disorienting.

Exploiting the Net

- **Approach Shots:** Incorporate approach shots into your strategy to transition to the net effectively. Successful approaches pressure your opponent and allow you to finish points with volleys or overheads, using the entire court to your advantage.
- **Serve and Volley:** Occasionally employing a serve-and-volley tactic can add an unexpected element to your game, keeping your opponent guessing and utilizing the forward part of the court.

Baseline Strategy

- **Cross-Court and Down the Line:** Mastering both cross-court and down-the-line shots from the baseline allows you to control the rally's direction. Alternating between these shots can move your opponent laterally and longitudinally, exploiting the full dimensions of the court.

Lob and Passing Shots

- **Defensive Lobs:** Use defensive lobs to counter net approaches by your opponent, pushing them back and regaining time to position yourself better.
- **Passing Shots:** Practice hitting passing shots when your opponent comes to the net, aiming for precision rather

than power to utilize the open spaces on the court.

Practice Drills for Court Utilization

- **Angle Creation Drill:** Set up targets in the corners and along the sidelines to practice creating wide angles with both forehand and backhand shots.
- **Depth Control Drill:** Practice hitting balls to designated deep and short areas of the court to work on your ability to vary shot depth effectively.
- **Net Play Simulation:** Work on approach shots followed by volleys and overheads, simulating the transition from baseline to net play.

Effectively utilizing the whole court requires a strategic mindset, technical skill in shot-making, and the physical ability to execute various shots under pressure. By developing these capabilities and consciously working to expand your use of the court in practice and match play, you can become a more versatile and formidable singles player, capable of outmaneuvering opponents with the strategic depth of your game.

DOUBLES DYNAMICS

The Key Differences Between Singles and Doubles

Transitioning from singles to doubles in tennis requires adjustments in strategy, positioning, and mentality. While the core skills of tennis remain vital in both formats, the dynamics of doubles introduce unique aspects that differentiate it significantly from singles play. Understanding these differences is crucial for players looking to excel in doubles matches. Here are the key distinctions between singles and doubles tennis:

Court Coverage and Positioning

- In doubles, the court is effectively wider due to the inclusion of the doubles alleys, requiring players to cover more lateral ground. Positioning becomes a strategic endeavor, with partners needing to coordinate their movements to cover the court efficiently without leaving gaps for opponents to exploit.

Teamwork and Communication

- Effective doubles play hinges on teamwork and clear communication between partners. Signals, verbal cues, and a mutual understanding of each other's playstyle are essential for coordinating serves, returns, and net play. This contrasts with singles, where decision-making and strategy are solely up to the individual player.

Serving and Return Strategies

- Doubles serving strategies must account for the presence of a net player on both sides, influencing where serves are directed and the types of serves used. Similarly, return strategies in doubles often involve aiming returns at specific areas of the court to neutralize the net player's advantage or to set up one's partner for a strong follow-up shot.

Net Play

- Net play is more prominent and crucial in doubles than in singles. Points in doubles are often won at the net, with both players frequently looking to move forward and control the net. Mastery of volleys, overheads, and reflex shots is essential, as is the ability to execute and defend against aggressive net play.

Shot Selection and Rally Tactic

- The tactical approach to shot selection in doubles differs due to the court dynamics and the presence of a partner. Lob shots, for instance, become a more strategic tool to move opponents out of favorable net positions. Cross-court shots, which are safer in singles due to the longer distance, carry a higher risk in doubles if they are not hit with precision due to the opponent's net player.

Mental and Psychological Dynamics

- Doubles introduces a shared mental and psychological component to the game, where partners must support each other, manage shared pressure, and collectively bounce back from setbacks. The partnership's dynamic can significantly influence performance, emphasizing the importance of a positive, supportive relationship between teammates.

Practice Adjustments for Doubles

- Players transitioning from singles to doubles should incorporate drills and practice scenarios that focus on these key differences. This includes practicing serves and returns with a focus on doubles positioning, engaging in volley and overhead drills, and playing practice points that emphasize teamwork and court coverage.

Understanding and adapting to the nuances of doubles play can enhance a player's versatility and overall tennis acumen. By embracing the strategic, positional, and psychological differences that doubles presents, players can enjoy the unique challenges and rewards that this format brings to the tennis court.

Communication and Teamwork

In doubles tennis, effective communication and seamless teamwork are not just beneficial; they are essential for success. The dynamic interplay between partners significantly influences the outcome of matches. A well-coordinated team can outmaneuver and outplay opponents who may be individually skilled but less synchronized. Here's how to cultivate communication and teamwork in doubles play:

Pre-Match Planning

- **Strategy Discussion:** Before the match, discuss strategies that leverage both partners' strengths and target opponents' weaknesses. Plan your serving, returning, and positioning tactics.
- **Signal Systems:** Establish a system of hand signals or verbal cues to communicate intentions for serves, poaching, and shot preferences. This covert communication ensures both partners are aligned on each point without tipping off opponents.

On-Court Communication

- **During Points:** Use quick, clear verbal cues ("Mine!" "Yours!" "Leave!" "Go!") during rallies to indicate who should take the ball. This reduces hesitation and overlap, allowing for more fluid play.
- **Changeovers and Breaks:** Utilize breaks in play to discuss adjustments to your game plan based on the match's flow. Open dialogue about what's working and what's not helps refine your strategy in real time.

Team Positioning and Movement

- **Moving as a Unit:** Practice moving in sync with your partner, maintaining an optimal distance that covers the court effectively. When one player moves to the net, the other should adjust their position accordingly, ensuring no part of the court is left undefended.
- **Covering for Each Other:** Be ready to cover more court if your partner is pulled out of position. Effective teams compensate for each other's movements, maintaining pressure on their opponents.

Supporting Each Other

- **Encouragement:** Stay positive and encourage your partner, especially after errors. Doubles play thrives on mutual support and shared confidence.
- **Managing Conflict:** Address disagreements or frustrations constructively. Focus on solutions and maintain a united front, as discord can be exploited by opponents.

Practice Drills for Teamwork

- **Coordination Drills:** Practice drills that emphasize coordinated movement, such as one partner hitting a lob while the other moves to the net, followed by synchronized net play.
- **Communication Drills:** Engage in drills that require constant communication, such as calling balls in or out for your partner or dictating play direction with verbal cues.
- **Scenario Simulations:** Play out specific match scenarios, focusing on how you and your partner adjust your strategy and positioning in response to different challenges.

The cultivation of communication and teamwork in doubles cannot be overstated. Teams that communicate effectively and move as a cohesive unit gain a strategic advantage and are capable of adapting to and overcoming the challenges presented by their opponents. By prioritizing these elements in practice and matches, doubles teams can enhance their synergy, making them more formidable and successful on the court.

Positioning and Court Coverage in Doubles

Positioning and court coverage are pivotal in doubles tennis, dictating a team's ability to defend their side and launch effective attacks. Unlike singles, where individual strategy and movement predominate, doubles requires a synchronized approach to covering the court, with partners working in tandem to maximize their defensive and offensive potential. Here's how to optimize positioning and court coverage in doubles play:

Basic Positioning Strategies

- **Both Up:** Both players are at the net to dominate the offensive play and reduce the opponents' angles for passing shots. This aggressive stance is effective for putting pressure on opponents, especially during serve-and-volley plays or when looking to close out points quickly.
- **Both Back:** Both players start from the baseline, a defensive setup that allows teams to handle powerful serves or groundstrokes more effectively. This position can be strategic when facing strong baseline opponents, providing more time to react and set up returns.
- **One Up, One Back:** One player is at the net and the other at the baseline, offering a balance between offense and defense. This flexible positioning allows the net player to intercept and put away weak returns while the baseline player covers deep shots.

Effective Court Coverage

- **Lateral Movement:** Partners should move laterally in sync, maintaining an imaginary line between them to cover the width of the court effectively. This coordination ensures that gaps are minimized, making it difficult for opponents to find open spaces.
- **Vertical Movement:** When one player moves forward to the net, the other should slightly adjust their position back and toward the center, ready to cover lobs or deeper shots. Conversely, if the net player retreats, the baseline player can move up to maintain pressure.
- **Switching and Poaching:** Successful doubles teams are adept at switching sides fluidly when necessary and

making calculated decisions to poach, intercepting the ball before it reaches their partner. Clear communication and trust are essential for executing these moves without compromising court coverage.

Communication and Signals

- Before each point, partners can use hand signals or verbal cues to indicate who will cover the middle, who might poach, or specific serve strategies. This pre-point planning helps prevent confusion and overlap during play.

Practice Drills for Positioning and Coverage

- **Mirror Drill:** Partners move laterally back and forth across the court in unison, practicing their ability to maintain an optimal distance between them.
- **Poaching Drills:** Practice drills where one player intentionally poaches to intercept returns, honing the timing and coordination required for effective net play.
- **Offensive and Defensive Transitions:** Set up points where teams must switch from both back to one up, one back, and both up positions, adapting their court coverage and strategies in response to the ball's play.

Mastering positioning and court coverage in doubles requires a blend of strategic understanding, dynamic coordination, and seamless communication between partners. By focusing on these aspects, doubles teams can significantly enhance their competitive edge, making it challenging for opponents to exploit gaps or predict their movements. Incorporating specific drills and strategies into practice sessions can further refine these skills, leading to improved performance and success in doubles matches.

Serving and Returning in Doubles

Serving and returning in doubles tennis involves strategic considerations distinct from singles play, largely due to the presence of a partner and the necessity to navigate against two opponents. The dynamics of the doubles game require teams to employ serving and returning strategies that maximize their strengths while exploiting their opponents' weaknesses. Here's how to approach serving and returning effectively in doubles:

Serving Strategies in Doubles

- **Placement Over Power:** While a powerful serve is advantageous, precise placement becomes even more critical in doubles. Serving to specific targets can set up the point for your team by putting the returner in a difficult position, allowing your net partner to poach effectively.
- **Variety:** Incorporate a mix of serves, including flat, slice, and kick serves, to keep opponents guessing. Varying the speed, spin, and direction of your serves can disrupt the returners' rhythm and prevent them from setting up strong returns.
- **Body Serves:** Utilizing serves directed at the body can be particularly effective in doubles, as they limit the returner's ability to create angles and may result in weaker returns that your net partner can capitalize on.

Returning Strategies in Doubles

- **Cross-Court Priority:** Due to the positioning of the players and the geometry of the court, cross-court returns are generally the safest and most strategic option in doubles. They reduce the risk of being intercepted by the net player and provide your team time to establish position.

- **Lob Returns:** When facing aggressive net players, lob returns can be a valuable tool to push them back and regain control of the net. Practice both defensive and offensive lobs to add depth to your returning game.
- **Aggressive Returns:** When the opportunity arises, particularly on second serves, stepping in to hit an aggressive return can shift the momentum in your favor. Aim for deep returns to limit the serving team's ability to attack and create openings for your team to take the offensive.

Communication and Coordination

- Before each point, discuss and signal where the serve will be directed and whether the net player intends to poach. This coordination ensures that both team members are prepared for the likely outcomes of the serve or return.
- Develop a system for quickly signaling intentions and adjusting strategies based on the success of previous serves or returns.

Practice Drills for Serving and Returning

- **Targeted Serving Drill:** Practice serving to specific areas of the box, focusing on placement and variation. Include scenarios where your partner poaches off your serve to simulate match conditions.
- **Return Positioning Drill:** Work on returning serves from different positions, adjusting for various types of serves. Practice cross-court and down-the-line returns, as well as lob returns, to cover all potential match scenarios.

- **Serve and Volley Drill:** In a doubles context, practice serving and immediately transitioning to the net. This drill helps the serving team work on their coordination and net coverage following the serve.

Effective serving and returning in doubles require a blend of individual skill, strategic planning, and team coordination. By focusing on placement, variety, and adapting to the evolving dynamics of the match, doubles teams can create pressure on their opponents, opening up opportunities to dominate points right from the serve or return. Incorporating specific drills and strategies into practice sessions will enhance these aspects of your doubles game, leading to more successful and dynamic play.

CASE STUDY: THE LEGENDARY BRYAN BROTHERS IN DOUBLES TENNIS

Bob and Mike Bryan, identical twins from the United States, have left an indelible mark on the world of doubles tennis, setting records that speak to their extraordinary synergy, skill, and sportsmanship. Their careers are filled with memorable matches that not only highlight their dominance in doubles tennis but also underscore the nuances of teamwork, communication, and strategy inherent in the format. Here's a look at one of their legendary matches and the turning points that define their legacy:

2012 Olympic Games Men's Doubles Final – Bryan/Bryan vs. Tsonga/Llodra

- **Background:** The Bryan brothers entered the 2012 Olympics in London with nearly every major title under their belts, except for Olympic gold. Facing the French team of Jo-Wilfried Tsonga and Michael Llodra, the Bryans had the chance to complete their "Golden Slam," winning all four Grand Slam titles and Olympic gold, a rare feat in tennis.

- **The Turning Point:** The match was tightly contested, with both teams showcasing exceptional skill. The critical moment came in the second set. After winning the first set, the Bryan brothers found themselves under pressure, with the French pair playing aggressively and pushing them to the brink. However, it was the Bryan brothers' unparalleled coordination and understanding of each other's play that proved decisive.

- **Strategic Adjustment:** Recognizing the need to disrupt their opponents' rhythm, the Bryans began to vary their service games and net play, incorporating more poaching and sharper angles. This strategic adjustment caught Tsonga and Llodra off-guard, allowing the Bryan brothers to secure crucial breaks.

- **Mental Resilience:** Beyond tactics, the Bryans' mental resilience shone through. Faced with the immense pressure of the occasion and the prospect of achieving a lifelong goal, they remained composed, communicating effectively and supporting one another through challenging moments.

- **Victory:** The Bryan brothers won the match in straight sets, cementing their place in tennis history by completing the career Golden Slam in doubles. Their joy and celebration upon winning were emblematic of their careers—marked by shared triumphs and a brotherly bond that transcended sport.

This match is a testament to the Bryan brothers' legendary status in doubles tennis. Their ability to adapt strategically, coupled with their unmatched chemistry and mental fortitude, made them not just champions on the court but also ambassadors of the doubles game. Through their career, Bob and Mike Bryan demonstrated that doubles tennis requires not just individual skill but a deep, intuitive connection between partners—a legacy that will inspire generations to come.

Having delved into the foundational elements of rallying for success, the intricacies of singles competition, and the collaborative dynamics of doubles play, it's clear that tennis is as much about strategy as it is about skill. But to truly elevate your game, understanding advanced strategies and tactics becomes paramount. These are the tools that allow you to not just react to the game as it unfolds but to shape the flow of play, anticipate your opponent's moves, and make calculated decisions that can turn the tide of a match in your favor.

As we transition into Chapter 6, "Advanced Strategies and Tactics," we will explore the nuanced aspects of tennis strategy that can give you a competitive edge. From exploiting specific match situations to adapting to special circumstances on the court, this chapter will refine your tactical game, enabling you to outthink and outplay your opponents with a sophisticated understanding of tennis at its highest level.

FREE GOODWILL

"When we share our love for the game, we give joy to others. Paying it forward, one racket at a time."

— UNKNOWN

The feeling of whacking a ball over the net or hitting the perfect serve is unmatched. You know, I know it. And guess what? When you give selflessly, you not only serve up joy, but you also receive a volley of happiness in return. So, if there's any chance of hitting that sweet spot during our tennis journey, count me in!

To do that, I have a question for you…

Would you help someone you've never met if it cost you nothing, but you never got credit for it?

Who is this person you ask? They are like you. Or, at least, like you used to be. Less experienced, wanting to become a better tennis player, and needing help, but not sure where to look.

My mission is to make tennis accessible to everyone. Everything I do stems from that mission. And, the only way for me to accomplish that mission is by reaching… well… *everyone.*

This is where you come in. Most people do, in fact, judge a book by its cover (and its reviews). So here's my ask on behalf of a struggling tennis player you've never met:

Please help that tennis player by leaving this book a review.

Your review costs no money and takes less than 60 seconds to make, but can change a fellow tennis player's life forever. Your review could help...

- ...one more kid feel the excitement of their first game.
- ...one more beginner get the hang of their backhand.
- ...one more parent bond with their child over a match.
- ...one more adult find a new, healthy hobby.
- ...one more person fall in love with the sport.

To get that 'feel good' feeling and help this person for real, all you have to do is... and it takes less than 60 seconds... leave a review.

Simply scan the QR code below to leave your review:

If you feel good about helping a faceless tennis player, you are my kind of person. Welcome to the club. You're one of us.

I'm that much more excited to help you become a better tennis player faster than you can possibly imagine. You'll love the tips and techniques I'm about to share in the coming chapters.

Thank you from the bottom of my heart. Now, back to Part 2 where we take your game to the next level.

Your biggest fan,

- Derek Drozd

PS - Fun fact: If you provide something of value to another person, it makes you more valuable to them. If you'd like goodwill straight from another tennis player - and you believe this book will help them - send this book their way.

Part Two

INTERMEDIATE TO ADVANCED PLAYERS – TAKING YOUR GAME TO THE NEXT LEVEL

ADVANCED STRATEGIES AND TACTICS

I magine a scenario where you are an underdog, facing a seemingly insurmountable opponent, but manage to turn the match around with a strategy so unexpected that it becomes the stuff of legend. Although underestimated and overlooked, you dive deep into the tactical playbook, finding a way to not just challenge but outmaneuver an opponent celebrated for their prowess. This journey to victory, fueled by the clever use of advanced strategies and tactics, underlines a profound truth in tennis: knowledge, when applied with precision and creativity, can level the playing field, turning perceived weaknesses into formidable strengths.

As we embark on Chapter 6, "Advanced Strategies and Tactics," let's uncover the layers of strategic depth in tennis, exploring how innovative thinking and tactical acumen can lead to triumphant outcomes against all odds. This chapter is a testament to the power of strategy, serving as a guide for players seeking to elevate their game beyond the conventional to a realm where every match is a chess game and every player has the potential to be a grandmaster.

MATCH PREPARATION AND GAME PLAN

Analyzing Your Opponent

Success in tennis often hinges on your ability to prepare effectively for each match, which includes developing a comprehensive understanding of your opponent's game. Analyzing your opponent isn't just about identifying their strengths and weaknesses; it's about recognizing patterns, preferences, and potential psychological edges. Here's how to approach opponent analysis to craft a winning game plan:

Technical Assessment

- **Strengths and Weaknesses:** Begin by evaluating your opponent's technical strengths (e.g., powerful serve, strong forehand) and weaknesses (e.g., vulnerable backhand, inconsistent net play). This assessment helps you identify which areas of their game you can exploit and which areas you should avoid engaging in directly.
- **Shot Preferences:** Observe their preferred shot selections in various situations. Some players favor topspin heavy forehands from the baseline, while others might opt for slice backhands as a defensive tactic.

Tactical Patterns

- **Serve Patterns:** Note their serving habits, including preferred serve spots on crucial points and their tendencies to hit flat, slice, or kick serves under different circumstances.
- **Rally Habits:** Pay attention to how they construct points during rallies. Look for patterns, such as always

approaching the net behind a deep forehand or frequently using drop shots to draw opponents forward.

Physical and Mental Condition

- **Endurance and Speed:** Assess their physical condition, focusing on their speed around the court and endurance in long matches. This information can inform strategies like extending rallies to wear them down or exploiting slower movement.
- **Mental Toughness:** Gauge their mental resilience by observing how they react to pressure situations, mistakes, and momentum shifts. Players who show signs of frustration or impatience can be targeted with strategies designed to apply psychological pressure.

Pre-Match Preparation

- **Video Analysis:** Whenever possible, review video footage of your opponent's previous matches to get a visual sense of their playing style and to confirm any patterns you've identified through other means.
- **Consultation and Scouting:** Speak with coaches, teammates, or players who have previously faced your opponent. First-hand insights can provide valuable information that complements your own observations.

Developing a Game Plan

- Based on your analysis, develop a tailored game plan that maximizes your strengths against their weaknesses. This plan should include specific tactics for serving, returning, point construction, and psychological warfare.

- Be prepared to adjust your game plan as the match progresses. Effective opponent analysis includes the ability to adapt to in-match changes, whether they're adjustments in your opponent's strategy or unforeseen conditions that impact play.

The process of analyzing your opponent and developing a game plan is a crucial aspect of match preparation in advanced tennis strategy. By thoroughly understanding your opponent's game and preparing accordingly, you position yourself to exploit their weaknesses, capitalize on your strengths, and navigate the mental and physical challenges of competitive play. This proactive approach to match preparation not only enhances your confidence heading into the match but also provides a strategic framework that can guide your decision-making on the court.

Developing a Match Strategy

Once you've analyzed your opponent, the next step is to develop a cohesive match strategy that leverages your strengths and exploits their weaknesses. A well-conceived strategy not only prepares you for the battle ahead but also provides a roadmap for making adjustments as the match unfolds. Here's how to approach developing an effective match strategy:

Establish Your Baseline Game

- **Play to Your Strengths:** Identify the aspects of your game that give you the most confidence—whether it's a powerful serve, a reliable groundstroke, or agility at the net. Plan to structure points around these strengths.
- **Neutralize Their Strengths:** Based on your opponent's analysis, devise ways to neutralize their most potent

weapons. This might involve avoiding their forehand, targeting their weaker backhand, or drawing them into uncomfortable positions.

Tactical Point Construction

- **Opening Points:** Start points with a purpose. Use your serve and return to immediately place your opponent under pressure or to set up patterns that favor your strengths.
- **Pattern Play:** Develop patterns of play that you can rely on under pressure. This might include a serve out wide followed by a forehand down the line or a deep return to set up a baseline rally that is advantageous to you.

Adaptability and Flexibility

- **Plan B and C:** Always have alternative strategies ready. If your primary game plan isn't working, be prepared to switch tactics. This might mean changing the pace of the game, varying shot heights and spins, or adopting a more aggressive or defensive posture.
- **In-Match Adjustments:** Stay alert to the need for adjustments based on the score, your opponent's adaptability, and changing conditions (e.g., wind, surface, fatigue). Being flexible allows you to stay one step ahead tactically.

Psychological Strategies

- **Mental Toughness:** Incorporate mental toughness strategies, like focusing on one point at a time and using positive self-talk, to maintain your competitive edge.

- **Applying Pressure:** Use strategic plays that put psychological pressure on your opponent, such as targeting their weaknesses at crucial moments or consistently forcing them to hit their least favorite shots.

Physical Considerations

- **Energy Management:** Plan your physical exertion to ensure you have the energy for critical stages of the match. This includes managing long rallies, deciding when to play aggressively, and recognizing moments where it's strategic to conserve energy.
- **Conditioning:** Tailor your strategy to match your physical conditioning. If you have superior endurance, consider strategies that extend points to wear down your opponent.

Practice Drills for Strategy Development

- **Scenario-Based Drills:** Practice drills that simulate specific match scenarios, adjusting your strategy based on the scenario's requirements. This helps improve decision-making under simulated match conditions.
- **Pattern Play Drills:** Work on drills that reinforce your preferred patterns of play, ensuring these patterns become second nature during matches.

Developing a match strategy is an evolving process that requires a deep understanding of your own game, a thorough analysis of your opponent, and the flexibility to adjust as the match progresses. By carefully crafting a strategy that plays to your strengths, mitigates your weaknesses, and puts your opponent under constant pressure, you position yourself for success on the court.

Adapting Your Game Plan Mid-Match

Tennis matches are dynamic, and the ability to adapt your game plan mid-match is crucial for overcoming challenges and seizing opportunities. Whether it's due to an opponent's unexpected strategy, changes in playing conditions, or fluctuations in your own performance, being able to adjust on the fly can be the difference between victory and defeat. Here's how to effectively adapt your game plan during a match:

Recognizing the Need for Adjustment

- **Monitor Effectiveness:** Regularly assess the effectiveness of your current strategy. Are you winning points as anticipated? Is your opponent consistently exploiting a weakness?
- **Watch for Opponent Adjustments:** Be alert to any changes in your opponent's tactics. An increase in aggression, a shift in targeting, or improved performance on previously weak shots may signal the need for you to adapt.
- **Acknowledge External Factors:** Weather conditions, court surface changes (in outdoor matches), or even crowd dynamics can influence match play. Be prepared to adjust your game plan to these external factors.

Strategies for Adaptation

- **Change Pace and Rhythm:** If your opponent is getting comfortable with the pace of the game, consider mixing up shot speeds and spins or adding more variety to disrupt their rhythm.

- **Alter Court Positioning:** Changing your position on the court, such as moving closer to the baseline for returns or approaching the net more frequently, can force your opponent to adjust their shot selection.
- **Focus on High-Percentage Tennis:** If errors are costing you points, refocus on high-percentage shots. Aim for deeper, safer targets on the court to reduce mistakes and build pressure on your opponent.
- **Exploit Opponent's Weaknesses:** If you discover a weakness in your opponent's game during the match, adjust your strategy to target this vulnerability more aggressively.

Communicating Adjustments

- **Solo Reflection:** In singles, use the changeovers to reflect on your performance and strategize adjustments. A mental reset can be as effective as a tactical one.
- **Partner Discussion:** In doubles, communicate openly with your partner about potential adjustments. Quick discussions can lead to effective changes in positioning, serving strategy, or target areas.

Implementing Changes Gradually

- **Test Adjustments:** Implement adjustments gradually to test their effectiveness without completely abandoning your initial strategy. This approach allows you to gauge the impact of changes without significant risk.
- **Stay Flexible:** Be willing to revert to your original plan or try alternative strategies if your adjustments do not yield the desired results. Flexibility is key to finding the most effective approach during a match.

Adapting your game plan mid-match requires a keen sense of awareness, the courage to make changes, and the wisdom to know when adjustments are necessary. By staying observant, flexible, and strategic, you can navigate the ebb and flow of match dynamics, positioning yourself for success regardless of the challenges that arise.

Importance of a Plan B

In the unpredictable arena of competitive tennis, having a Plan B is not just prudent; it's essential. No matter how well you analyze your opponent or how perfectly you devise your initial strategy, the dynamic nature of the game means things won't always go according to plan. Injuries, unanticipated opponent adjustments, or even your own off-day can render your primary strategy ineffective. Here's why having a Plan B is critical and how it can serve as your safety net during matches:

Psychological Safety Net

- **Boosts Confidence:** Knowing you have a fallback strategy can boost your confidence, allowing you to play more freely and with less fear of the unknown. It reassures you that there are options to turn the match around if things don't initially go your way.
- **Reduces Pressure:** A Plan B can alleviate the pressure to execute your primary strategy perfectly, helping you maintain mental composure even when faced with adversity.

Tactical Flexibility

- **Adaptability to Conditions:** External conditions such as weather, court surface, and even crowd dynamics can influence the effectiveness of your game plan. A Plan B provides the tactical flexibility to adapt your play style to these changing conditions.
- **Counteracting Opponent Adjustments:** If your opponent manages to neutralize your primary strategy, having an alternative approach allows you to shift tactics, keeping them off-balance and reclaiming control of the match dynamics.

Overcoming Performance Variability

- **Adjusting for Off-Days:** Even elite athletes have days when certain aspects of their game are not at their best. A Plan B allows you to shift focus to the parts of your game that are working well on that particular day.
- **Coping With Injuries or Fatigue:** Minor injuries or fatigue can limit your ability to execute your primary strategy. An alternative plan that accounts for these limitations can be crucial for staying competitive.

Developing and Implementing a Plan B

- **Strategic Depth:** Your Plan B should still play to your strengths but in a way that differs from your main strategy. This might involve changing from an aggressive baseline game to more net play, focusing on consistency over power, or vice versa.
- **Practice Variability:** Incorporate your Plan B into practice sessions to ensure you're as comfortable and

confident with it as you are with your primary strategy. This includes drilling different shot selections, tactics, and mental approaches.

- **In-Match Signals:** Establish signals or cues with your coach (for allowed events) or mental markers for yourself to recognize when it might be time to switch to your Plan B. Being able to make this decision promptly can be pivotal in closely contested matches.

Embracing Plan B as Part of Your Game

- Recognize that switching to a Plan B is not an admission of failure but a strategic adjustment that showcases your versatility and tactical acumen. The best players are those who can navigate through a match's ebb and flow, utilizing every tool at their disposal to secure victory.

Having a well-thought-out Plan B empowers you to enter each match with a broader strategic outlook, ready to tackle whatever challenges arise. This level of preparation and adaptability not only enhances your chances of success but also contributes to your growth as a resilient and strategic-minded player.

SPECIAL SITUATIONS AND ADAPTATIONS

Playing Against Different Types of Players

Tennis is a sport of diverse playing styles, and success often hinges on your ability to adapt your game to counteract various types of opponents effectively. Whether facing a powerful baseliner, a crafty counterpuncher, a net-rushing serve-and-volleyer, or a consistent ball machine, understanding the strengths and weaknesses of different styles and knowing how to adjust your strategy accordingly can give you a competitive edge. Here's how to adapt your game plan when playing against different types of players:

The Power Baseliner

- **Strategy:** Neutralize their power by increasing the depth of your shots, aiming to push them back and reduce their angle of attack. Incorporate slice shots to disrupt their rhythm and employ high topspin shots to their weaker side to force errors.
- **Adaptation:** Stay patient and focus on constructing points carefully. Utilize lobs and passing shots when they approach the net and aim to exploit any lack of mobility.

The Counterpuncher

- **Strategy:** Counterpunchers excel at defensive play and returning balls that would typically win points. To overcome this, vary your shot pace and spin to draw them out of their comfort zone. Use drop shots to bring them to the net, and follow up with lob or angled shots to catch them off guard.
- **Adaptation:** Avoid unforced errors by playing high-percentage tennis. Be prepared for long rallies, and focus on patiently waiting for openings to attack decisively.

The Serve-and-Volleyer

- **Strategy:** Direct your returns low at their feet to complicate their volley attempts. Incorporate passing shots and lobs into your game to keep them guessing. Returning deep and at angles can also prevent them from setting up comfortable volleys.

- **Adaptation:** Improve your reaction time to fast serves and practice blocking returns back into play. Position yourself slightly back during their serve to give yourself more time to react.

The Slicer

- **Strategy:** Players who frequently use slice shots can disrupt your rhythm with low-bouncing balls. Counter this by stepping into the court to take the ball on the rise, maintaining depth in your shots to push them back. High topspin shots to their backhand can also be effective.
- **Adaptation:** Maintain a flexible knee bend to effectively handle low shots. Stay patient, and don't rush your shots, as slicers often rely on opponents' errors to win points.

The All-Court Player

- **Strategy:** All-court players are versatile and can adapt their game as needed. To compete against them, you must be equally adaptable, changing tactics mid-match if necessary. Focus on exploiting any subtle weaknesses they may have and playing to your strengths.
- **Adaptation:** Monitor the effectiveness of your strategies closely and be ready to switch tactics. For example, if they handle baseline rallies well, consider incorporating more net play into your game.

Practice Drills for Adaptability

- **Versatile Opponent Drills:** Practice with partners who can simulate different playing styles. This exposure will help you adjust your game to various opponents.
- **Specific Scenario Training:** Set up drills that focus on countering specific strategies, such as returning serve-and-volley plays or handling heavy topspin shots.

Adapting your play to effectively counter different types of opponents is a skill that develops with experience, analysis, and intentional practice. By understanding the nuances of various playing styles and preparing strategies to neutralize their strengths, you can enhance your ability to compete successfully against a wide range of players, making you a more versatile and formidable tennis competitor.

Adjusting to Various Court Surfaces

Tennis is unique among sports for the variety of playing surfaces it offers, each with its own characteristics that can significantly affect the game's dynamics. From the slow, high-bouncing clay to the fast, low-skimming grass courts and the medium-paced hard courts, adapting your game to suit the surface you're playing on is a crucial skill. Here's how to adjust your strategy and technique for various court surfaces:

Clay Courts

- **Strategy Adjustment:** Clay courts slow down the ball and produce a higher bounce, favoring baseline rallies and players who excel in consistency and spin. Build points patiently, use heavy topspin to push opponents back, and be prepared for longer rallies.

- **Movement Adaptation:** Sliding into shots is a key movement on clay, allowing for efficient recovery and positioning. Practice sliding correctly to prevent injury and improve court coverage.

Grass Courts

- **Strategy Adjustment:** Grass courts favor fast play, with the ball skimming low off the surface. Serve-and-volley tactics, along with slice shots that stay low, can be particularly effective. Aim for quick points, using flat, powerful shots to rush your opponent.
- **Movement Adaptation:** Quick, short steps are essential on grass to adjust to the ball's unpredictable bounces. Work on your agility and reaction time to adapt to the faster pace of play.

Hard Courts

- **Strategy Adjustment:** Hard courts offer a balance between the speed of grass and the slowness of clay, accommodating a wide range of playing styles. Adapt your strategy based on your strengths and your opponent's weaknesses, whether that means powerful baseline rallies, aggressive net play, or a mix of both.
- **Movement Adaptation:** Hard courts can be tough on the body, so efficient footwork and proper shoes with good support and cushioning are important to prevent injury.

Indoor Courts

- **Strategy Adjustment:** Indoor courts typically have a consistent, medium-fast pace and are not subject to outdoor elements like wind or sun. This consistency can favor players with a strong serve or those who excel in precision and control. Use the controlled conditions to play a high-precision game.
- **Movement Adaptation:** Movement on indoor courts is similar to hard courts, but the lack of external factors means you can focus more on your technique and less on adjusting for wind or lighting conditions.

Practice Tips for Surface Adaptation

- **Surface-Specific Drills:** Whenever possible, practice on the surface you'll be competing on. Focus on drills that enhance the skills and strategies most effective for that surface.
- **Mental Adaptation:** Prepare mentally for the pace and style of play typical of the surface. Visualization and strategic planning can help adjust your mindset and expectations.
- **Equipment Adjustments:** Tailor your equipment, especially your footwear, to the surface. Different surfaces require different types of traction and cushioning for optimal performance and safety.

Adjusting to various court surfaces requires a blend of strategic, technical, and mental adaptations. By understanding the unique characteristics of each surface and preparing accordingly, you can maximize your performance and enjoy a competitive edge, regardless of where your matches take place.

Weather Conditions and Their Impact

Weather conditions can significantly affect tennis play, influencing everything from ball behavior to player performance. Adapting to these conditions is a crucial skill, allowing players to maintain effectiveness and a competitive edge regardless of the weather. Here's how to adjust your game for various weather conditions:

Wind

- **Strategy Adjustment:** In windy conditions, play a higher margin game by reducing risk in your shots and aiming for the center of the court to avoid unforced errors. Use the wind to your advantage by hitting deeper, higher balls, which can be more challenging for your opponent to time correctly.
- **Technique Adaptation:** Shorten your swing on more gusty shots to maintain control. Serving and lobbing can be particularly tricky, so practice adjusting your toss and shot trajectory to compensate for wind direction and speed.

Sun and Heat

- **Strategy Adjustment:** In hot conditions, conserving energy becomes critical. Focus on winning points more efficiently, possibly through serve-and-volley tactics or by targeting your opponent's weaknesses to shorten rallies. Using high topspin shots can also increase your opponent's movement, wearing them down faster in the heat.
- **Physical Adaptation:** Stay hydrated and use changeovers to cool down with ice packs or cooling towels. Wear sunscreen and a hat or visor to protect against sun

exposure. Conditioning for heat tolerance through heat acclimatization training can also be beneficial.

Cold

- **Strategy Adjustment:** Cold weather can make the ball feel harder and less responsive, often resulting in slower speeds and lower bounces. Adjust by hitting with more force and using flat shots to maintain depth. The cold can also affect muscle flexibility, making it essential to keep moving and stay engaged in the match.
- **Equipment and Apparel Adaptation:** Use balls designed for colder temperatures if available. Wear layers that can be easily added or removed to maintain optimal body temperature without restricting movement.

Humidity

- **Strategy Adjustment:** Humid conditions can make the ball heavier and slower, impacting serve and shot speed. Adapt by focusing on spin and placement over power, and be prepared for longer rallies as the ball becomes more challenging to put away.
- **Physical Adaptation:** Manage hydration carefully as sweating increases in humid conditions. Utilize quick-dry clothing and grips to manage excess moisture.

Practice Tips for Weather Adaptation

- **Variable Weather Practice:** Whenever possible, practice in various weather conditions to become accustomed to adjusting your game accordingly. This experience is invaluable for building confidence and versatility.

- **Mental Flexibility:** Cultivate a mindset that views weather challenges as part of the game's unpredictability and excitement. Being mentally adaptable helps maintain focus and a positive attitude, regardless of conditions.
- **Equipment Preparedness:** Always come to matches prepared with the right equipment for weather conditions, including appropriate clothing, extra grips, and any additional gear needed for extreme temperatures or moisture.

Adapting to weather conditions requires a combination of strategic adjustments, physical preparedness, and mental flexibility. By recognizing the impact of different weather scenarios on play and preparing accordingly, players can ensure they remain competitive and capable of performing their best, no matter what Mother Nature has in store.

CASE STUDY: THE ADVANCED PRECISION OF NOVAK DJOKOVIC

Novak Djokovic, a name that stands tall in the realm of tennis, is renowned for his extraordinary baseline play, which is marked by unparalleled precision, control, and elasticity. Novak Djokovic's extraordinary tennis career is a saga of meticulous analysis, strategic brilliance, and the capacity to adapt fluidly to the demands of each match. This case study delves into the ways Djokovic has utilized his deep understanding of opponents' playing styles, his strategic planning for each match, and his ability to adapt mid-game to secure victory after victory, thus cementing his status as one of the sport's all-time greats.

Rise to Dominance and Career Milestones

- Djokovic turned professional in 2003, and after several years of steady progress, he began his rise to the upper echelons of the sport. His breakthrough came with his first Grand Slam title at the Australian Open in 2008. Since then, Djokovic has accumulated 20 Grand Slam singles titles, equaling the record for the most won by a male player, and has held the world No. 1 spot in the ATP rankings for over 300 weeks.

Analyzing Opponents

- **Pre-Match Preparation:** Djokovic's pre-match routine includes a thorough analysis of his opponents' recent matches. He studies their tendencies, strengths, weaknesses, and preferences, seeking to understand their strategies and anticipate their choices on the court. This preparation allows Djokovic to enter every match with a tailored plan of attack.
- **On-Court Analysis**: During matches, Djokovic continuously observes and analyzes his opponents' behavior, adjusting his tactics in response to their strategies. This real-time analysis is critical to his ability to make swift and effective tactical decisions.

Developing Match Strategy

- **Versatile Game Plan**: Djokovic's game plan often involves a balance of aggressive baseline play and strategic net approaches. He uses his deep groundstrokes and acute angles to control the rally, waiting for an opportunity to strike with precision.

- **Service Strategy**: Djokovic's serve has evolved into a formidable weapon, and he strategically varies its speed, placement, and spin to keep his opponents guessing and off-balance.
- **Mental and Physical Endurance**: Part of Djokovic's strategic approach includes his incredible physical endurance and mental fortitude, allowing him to engage in lengthy rallies and physically demanding matches while maintaining focus and performance under pressure.

Adapting When Necessary

- **Tactical Flexibility:** Beyond his technical prowess, Djokovic's strategic understanding of the game sets him apart. He excels in constructing points, exploiting opponents' weaknesses, and adapting his game plan mid-match to counter varying styles of play.
- **Responding to Adversity:** Djokovic is known for his resilience in facing adversity, whether it's a hostile crowd, an inspired opponent, or challenging weather conditions. His willingness to adapt his mental approach and maintain composure has been key to many of his comeback victories.

Legacy and Impact

- Novak Djokovic's legacy is one of intellectual and physical mastery of tennis. His analytical approach to understanding opponents, combined with his strategic acumen and adaptability on the court, have earned him a reputation as a cerebral champion. He has redefined what it means to be a complete player in the modern era, combining technical precision, athletic prowess, and a tactical mindset that transcends the sport. His career serves as a blueprint for success through continuous learning, adaptation, and the relentless pursuit of excellence.

With our exploration of strategies and tactics now refined and understanding how to adapt to a variety of opponents and situations, the next step in elevating your tennis game is to focus on the bedrock of any successful player: training and practice routines. Mastery in tennis doesn't occur in matches alone but is built on the foundation of disciplined, intelligent, and purposeful practice. As we transition into Chapter 7, "Training and Practice Routines," we will delve into the essential drills, exercises, and routines designed to keep your game sharp, improve your physical conditioning, and ensure that your strategic adaptations are not just theoretical but executable under the pressures of competitive play. This chapter is dedicated to providing you with the tools and insights necessary to refine your skills, enhance your endurance, and perfect your mental game, making sure that every aspect of your tennis is as effective and competitive as possible.

COMPETITIVE PLAY

I magine yourself struggling to break through the ranks, then deciding to dedicate an entire off-season to transforming your game. This isn't about minor tweaks or casual hitting sessions; it is a complete overhaul, encompassing rigorous physical conditioning, relentless skill refinement, and a deep dive into strategic understanding. Through disciplined training and practice routines, you not only elevate your game but also reshape your career trajectory, emerging as a formidable force on tour.

As we embark on Chapter 7, "Competitive Play," let's uncover the secrets behind effective training strategies that have the power to transform potential into excellence. This chapter is a guide to developing the work ethic, discipline, and strategic approach to practice that can turn ambitious goals into tangible success.

DEVELOPING A PERSONALIZED TRAINING PLAN

Assessing Your Strengths and Weaknesses

The foundation of any effective training plan in tennis—or any sport—is a clear, honest assessment of your strengths and weaknesses. This self-evaluation guides the customization of your training regimen, ensuring that it addresses areas needing improvement while further enhancing your strengths. Here's how to conduct this assessment and use it to inform your personalized training plan:

Technical Skills Assessment

- **Baseline Play:** Evaluate your forehand and backhand for consistency, power, and accuracy. Determine whether you struggle more with generating pace, maintaining control, or using spin effectively.
- **Net Game:** Assess your volleys and overheads, considering your comfort level at the net, shot precision, and reflexes.
- **Serve:** Analyze your serve for speed, accuracy, and variety. Identify if your second serve is a vulnerability that opponents can exploit.
- **Return:** Evaluate your return of serve for reliability, aggressiveness, and adaptability to different serve styles.

Physical Conditioning

- **Endurance:** Assess your ability to maintain a high level of play over long matches. Consider whether fatigue affects your shot quality or movement in later sets.
- **Speed and Agility:** Determine if your movement around

the court is a strength or if improving your speed and agility could significantly enhance your game.

- **Strength and Power:** Evaluate whether a lack of strength limits your shot power or if increased muscular endurance could improve your performance.

Tactical Awareness

- **Match Strategy:** Reflect on your ability to develop and stick to effective game plans. Consider your adaptability in matches and whether you struggle to adjust tactics as needed.
- **Mental Toughness:** Assess your mental resilience during matches, including your ability to stay focused, handle pressure, and recover from setbacks.

Using Feedback

- **Coach and Peer Feedback:** Incorporate feedback from coaches, training partners, and competitors. External perspectives can provide insights into areas you might overlook.
- **Match Analysis:** Review match footage, if available, to identify patterns in your play, especially during crucial points or when facing specific challenges.

Setting Priorities

- **Immediate Needs vs. Long-Term Goals:** Based on your assessment, prioritize areas for immediate improvement while also considering long-term developmental goals. Balancing short-term fixes with the pursuit of overarching skills ensures steady progress.

Developing the Plan

- **Customized Drills and Exercises:** Tailor your practice routines to focus on identified weaknesses, incorporating drills that specifically target these areas. Simultaneously, design drills to maintain and enhance your strengths.
- **Physical Training Regimen:** Include physical conditioning tailored to your needs, focusing on endurance, strength, agility, or a combination thereof, based on your assessment.
- **Mental Training:** Incorporate mental training techniques, such as visualization, positive self-talk, and pressure simulation drills, to improve your mental game.

Assessing your strengths and weaknesses is a critical first step in developing a personalized training plan that addresses your specific needs. By systematically evaluating every aspect of your game and using this information to guide your training focus, you can create a comprehensive, effective plan that promotes continuous improvement and prepares you for competitive success.

RECOVERY AND INJURY PREVENTION

Importance of Rest and Recovery

In the relentless pursuit of improvement and competitive excellence, rest and recovery are often undervalued elements of a tennis player's regimen. However, they are as crucial to performance as any drill, exercise, or practice match. Proper rest and recovery not only prevent injuries but also enhance physical and mental performance, ensuring that players can train and compete at their best over the long term. Here's why rest and recovery hold paramount importance:

Physical Restoration

- **Muscle Repair:** Intense training and competition place significant stress on the body, causing microtears in muscle fibers. Rest allows these fibers to repair and grow stronger, a process essential for improving strength and endurance.
- **Energy Replenishment:** Recovery periods help restore glycogen stores, the primary energy source for high-intensity activities like tennis. Adequate rest ensures you have the energy reserves needed for peak performance in both practice and matches.

Injury Prevention

- **Overuse Injuries:** Tennis, with its repetitive movements and impact, poses a risk for overuse injuries. Regular rest prevents the cumulative stress on muscles, tendons, and joints that can lead to injuries such as tendinitis or stress fractures.
- **Acute Injuries:** Fatigue can impair judgment, reaction times, and coordination, increasing the risk of acute injuries. Well-rested players are more alert and can maintain the proper technique and court positioning, reducing the likelihood of injury.

Mental Health and Performance

- **Psychological Resilience:** Rest and recovery contribute to mental well-being. Overtraining can lead to burnout, decreased motivation, and increased anxiety or stress. Adequate rest helps maintain a positive mental outlook and sharp focus.

- **Cognitive Function:** Rest, especially sufficient sleep, is crucial for cognitive functions such as memory, decision-making, and reaction times—all vital for strategic thinking and effective play on the court.

Enhancing Adaptation

- **Supercompensation:** The body adapts to the stress of training through a process called supercompensation, where it rebuilds itself to be stronger than before. This process occurs during rest periods, underscoring the importance of recovery in physical development.
- **Optimal Performance:** Rest is when the benefits of training consolidate. Without adequate recovery, the body cannot fully adapt to the stresses of training, potentially leading to performance plateaus or declines.

Strategies for Effective Recovery

- **Active Recovery:** Low-intensity activities, such as walking, swimming, or yoga, can promote recovery by increasing blood flow to muscles without placing additional stress on the body.
- **Sleep:** Prioritize sleep as a key component of recovery. Aim for 7–9 hours per night to facilitate physical repair and cognitive restoration.
- **Nutrition and Hydration:** Adopt a recovery-focused nutrition strategy, emphasizing protein intake for muscle repair, carbohydrates for energy replenishment, and adequate hydration to support overall health.

Monitoring and Adjusting Recovery Needs

- **Listen to Your Body:** Be attentive to signs of fatigue, soreness, or reduced performance, as these may indicate the need for additional rest.
- **Adjust Training Load:** Regularly assess and adjust your training volume and intensity based on recovery status, using tools like heart rate variability (HRV) monitoring to gauge readiness for training.

Emphasizing the importance of rest and recovery within a training and competition schedule is essential for sustained athletic performance, injury prevention, and overall well-being. By integrating deliberate recovery strategies and prioritizing rest, tennis players can ensure they remain physically and mentally prepared to meet the demands of their sport.

Common Tennis Injuries and How to Avoid Them

Tennis is a physically demanding sport that can lead to a variety of injuries, especially if proper precautions are not taken. By understanding the most common tennis injuries and implementing strategies to avoid them, players can enjoy a healthier, more sustainable career. Here's a look at frequent injuries in tennis and tips on how to prevent them:

Tennis Elbow (Lateral Epicondylitis)

- **Description:** A condition characterized by pain on the outside of the elbow, often due to overuse of the forearm muscles and tendons.
- **Prevention:** Strengthen forearm muscles through specific exercises, ensure proper racket grip size and string

tension, and use correct stroke mechanics to reduce strain on the elbow.

Rotator Cuff Injuries

- **Description:** Injuries to the rotator cuff, a group of muscles and tendons that stabilize the shoulder, can range from inflammation to tears. These injuries are often the result of repetitive overhead motions.
- **Prevention:** Strengthen shoulder stabilizer muscles, practice proper serving and overhead techniques, and incorporate regular shoulder flexibility exercises into your routine.

Ankle Sprains

- **Description:** An ankle sprain occurs when the ligaments that support the ankle stretch beyond their limits or tear. Quick changes in direction or uneven surfaces can increase the risk.
- **Prevention:** Improve ankle strength and stability through exercises like calf raises and balance drills. Wear supportive tennis shoes designed for lateral movement, and consider ankle braces if you have a history of sprains.

Stress Fractures

- **Description:** Stress fractures are tiny cracks in a bone, often occurring in the lower leg or foot from overuse and repetitive impact.
- **Prevention:** Gradually increase training intensity and volume, ensure adequate calcium and vitamin D intake for

bone health, and use shock-absorbing insoles or orthotics if recommended.

Patellar Tendinitis (Jumper's Knee)

- **Description:** Inflammation of the tendon connecting the kneecap to the shinbone, common in sports requiring frequent jumping or rapid changes in direction.
- **Prevention:** Strengthen quadriceps and hamstring muscles to better support the knee, incorporate plyometric exercises to improve tendon resilience, and stretch regularly to maintain flexibility.

Wrist Injuries

- **Description:** Wrist injuries can range from tendonitis to sprains and are often due to poor technique or overuse in wrist-intensive shots like the backhand.
- **Prevention:** Strengthen wrist and forearm muscles, ensure proper technique in all strokes, and consider wrist supports if experiencing pain or discomfort.

Back Injuries

- **Description:** Back injuries in tennis players can include muscle strains, ligament sprains, and disc injuries, often resulting from repetitive twisting and extension motions.
- **Prevention:** Strengthen core muscles to support the lower back, practice proper form during all strokes to minimize stress on the back, and incorporate flexibility exercises targeting the back and hips.

General Prevention Tips

- **Warm-Up Thoroughly:** Always perform a dynamic warm-up before playing to prepare your muscles and joints for the demands of tennis.
- **Cool Down and Stretch:** After playing, cool down with light aerobic activity followed by stretching to aid in recovery and flexibility.
- **Rest and Recovery:** Prioritize rest days and active recovery sessions to allow your body time to heal and prevent overuse injuries.
- **Hydration and Nutrition:** Maintain proper hydration and a balanced diet to support overall health and injury prevention.

Understanding these common tennis injuries and implementing preventive strategies can significantly reduce the risk of injury, allowing players to focus on improving their game and enjoying competition.

Stretching and Cool-Down Exercises

Adequately cooling down and stretching after playing tennis is essential for recovery, injury prevention, and maintaining flexibility. This process helps to gradually reduce heart rate, prevent muscle stiffness, and enhance overall mobility, contributing to a quicker recovery and readiness for future activities. Here are key stretching and cool-down exercises tailored for tennis players:

Cool-Down Routine

- Begin with a light aerobic activity to gradually lower your heart rate. This could include a gentle jog around the court, walking, or easy cycling for 5–10 minutes. The goal is to transition your body to a resting state smoothly.

Dynamic Stretching

- After the initial cool-down, incorporate dynamic stretches that involve gentle movement and mimic the motions used in tennis. These can include arm swings, hip circles, and gentle torso twists. Perform each movement for 30 seconds to 1 minute.

Static Stretching

Focus on static stretches, holding each position for at least 20–30 seconds to improve flexibility and relax muscles. Key areas to target include:

- **Forearm and Wrist Stretches:** Essential for players to counteract the grip tension from holding the racket. Extend one arm in front of you, palm down, and gently pull the fingers back with the other hand. Repeat with the palm facing up.
- **Shoulder Stretch:** Bring one arm across your body and use the other hand to press it into your chest, stretching the shoulder. Repeat on the other side.
- **Triceps Stretch:** Reach one hand down the center of your back, with your elbow pointing upward, and gently press on the elbow with the other hand to deepen the stretch.
- **Quadriceps Stretch:** Standing on one leg, pull the opposite heel toward your buttocks, keeping your knees together and pushing your hips forward.
- **Hamstring Stretch:** Sit on the ground with your legs extended. Reach toward your toes, keeping your back

straight. For a gentler stretch, bend the untargeted leg, placing the sole of the foot against the inner thigh of the extended leg.

- **Calf Stretch:** Place one foot behind the other and gently press the back heel down while keeping the leg straight, then bend the back knee slightly to target the Achilles tendon.
- **Hip and Glute Stretch:** Sit with one leg crossed over the other leg's thigh and gently pull the knee toward the opposite shoulder to stretch the hip and gluteal muscles.
- **Lower Back Stretch:** Lying on your back, pull your knees to your chest and gently rock side to side, then extend one leg and pull the other knee toward the opposite shoulder to stretch the lower back and glutes.

Incorporating Flexibility Tools

- Use foam rollers or massage balls to perform self-myofascial release on tight muscles, especially targeting the legs, back, and shoulders. This can help alleviate muscle knots and improve blood circulation.

Consistency Is Key

- Make stretching and cooling down a consistent part of your training routine. Regularity is crucial for reaping the long-term benefits of increased flexibility, reduced soreness, and injury prevention.

By dedicating time to a comprehensive cool-down and stretching routine after playing, tennis players can enhance their recovery process, maintain and improve flexibility, and prepare their bodies for the demands of future training sessions or matches.

Role of Physiotherapy and Massage

Physiotherapy and massage are integral components of a comprehensive approach to recovery, injury prevention, and overall physical maintenance for tennis players. Both modalities offer unique benefits that can enhance a player's ability to perform at their best, recover more efficiently from the rigors of training and competition, and prevent the onset of injuries. Understanding the role and benefits of physiotherapy and massage can help players incorporate these practices into their routines effectively.

Physiotherapy

- **Injury Prevention and Management:** A physiotherapist can identify potential risk factors for injury based on a player's movement patterns, technique, and muscle imbalances. Through targeted exercises and interventions, physiotherapy can address these risks, reducing the likelihood of injury.
- **Rehabilitation:** For players recovering from injuries, physiotherapy provides structured rehabilitation programs designed to safely return the athlete to play. These programs focus on restoring strength, flexibility, and function to injured areas while gradually reintroducing tennis-specific movements.
- **Performance Enhancement:** Physiotherapists can work with players to optimize their physical conditioning, focusing on areas such as mobility, stability, and proprioception. Enhancements in these areas can lead to improvements in on-court performance, including better shot execution and endurance.

Massage

- **Muscle Recovery:** Massage therapy helps accelerate the recovery process by increasing blood flow to the muscles, which can aid in the removal of metabolic waste products accumulated during intense physical activity. This can reduce muscle soreness and expedite the recovery of muscle function.
- **Flexibility and Range of Motion:** Regular massage can improve flexibility and range of motion by relieving muscle tension and breaking down scar tissue. This is particularly beneficial for tennis players, who rely on a wide range of motion for effective stroke play.
- **Stress Reduction and Mental Benefits:** Beyond physical benefits, massage therapy offers psychological benefits, including stress reduction and enhanced relaxation. A relaxed body and mind can contribute to improved focus and mental resilience on the court.
- **Injury Rehabilitation:** Massage can be part of an injury rehabilitation program, complementing physiotherapy and other treatments. Techniques such as deep tissue massage can target specific areas of injury or tension, promoting healing and reducing recovery time.

Incorporating Physiotherapy and Massage Into Your Routine

- **Regular Assessments:** Work with a physiotherapist for regular assessments, particularly during periods of heavy training or competition, to monitor physical condition and address any emerging issues proactively.
- **Post-Match Recovery:** Consider scheduling massage sessions following matches or intense practice sessions as

part of your recovery routine. Even a short, targeted massage can yield significant benefits.

- **Injury Recovery:** In the event of an injury, engage with both physiotherapy and massage as recommended by healthcare professionals to support efficient and effective recovery, ensuring a safe return to tennis.
- **Preventative Maintenance:** Don't wait for injuries to occur. Utilize physiotherapy and massage as preventative measures to maintain optimal physical condition and reduce the risk of injury.

The role of physiotherapy and massage in a tennis player's training regimen cannot be overstated. By providing physical and psychological benefits, these practices are essential for maintaining peak performance, ensuring longevity in the sport, and fostering overall well-being.

Coping With Injuries and Playing Through Pain

Injuries and pain are unfortunate realities of competitive tennis, often testing a player's resilience and adaptability. While playing through pain is sometimes possible, it's crucial to approach such situations with caution, prioritizing long-term health over short-term gains. Here's how to cope with injuries and manage pain while minimizing risk:

Understanding the Difference Between Pain and Injury

- **Pain as a Warning:** Learn to differentiate between normal muscle soreness due to exertion and pain that signals a potential injury. Pain that increases with activity or affects movement patterns significantly should be treated with caution.

- **Seek Professional Assessment:** Before deciding to play through pain, consult with a medical professional to understand the nature and severity of your injury. This assessment can guide your decision on whether and how to continue playing.

Adaptations and Adjustments

- **Modify Your Technique:** Depending on the nature of your injury, slight modifications to your technique or playing style may reduce pain and prevent further injury. For example, adjust your serve technique to minimize stress on an injured shoulder.
- **Strategic Gameplay Adjustments:** Alter your strategy to shorten points and conserve energy. This could involve more aggressive play, such as increased net approaches or using more drop shots and lobs to move your opponent around without exerting yourself excessively.

Physical Support and Protection

- **Use Protective Gear:** Braces, tapes, or compression garments can provide support and stability to injured areas, reducing pain during play. Ensure these aids are applied correctly to avoid restricting movement or causing further injury.
- **Physical Therapy and Conditioning:** Engage in physical therapy and targeted conditioning exercises to strengthen the muscles around the injured area, supporting recovery and preventing future injuries.

Pain Management Techniques

- **Proper Warm-Up and Cool-Down:** A thorough warm-up increases blood flow to muscles, reducing the risk of injury, while a proper cool-down can aid in recovery. Incorporate stretching and mobility exercises specific to your injury.
- **Pain Relief Methods:** Explore non-medical pain relief methods such as ice, heat therapy, or massage to manage discomfort before and after matches. Always consult with a healthcare provider before using pain relief medications, especially if they could mask injury symptoms.

Mental and Emotional Considerations

- **Maintain a Positive Outlook:** Focus on what you can control, including your attitude and effort. A positive mindset can influence pain perception and enhance your ability to cope with discomfort.
- **Listen to Your Body:** Be honest with yourself about your pain levels and the impact on your play. It's essential to recognize that continuing to play could lead to more severe injury and longer recovery times.

Practice and Competition Considerations

- **Practice Modifications:** Adjust practice intensity and duration to accommodate your injury, focusing on technique and low-impact exercises.
- **Competition Decisions:** Carefully consider the importance of upcoming matches and the potential impact of competition on your injury. Sometimes, rest and recovery are the best strategies for long-term success.

Coping with injuries and playing through pain requires a careful balance between competitive desire and health preservation. By making informed decisions, adapting your game, and focusing on recovery, you can manage injuries effectively while continuing to enjoy competitive tennis. Prioritizing your well-being ensures that you can return to your highest level of play as quickly and safely as possible.

CASE STUDY: VENUS WILLIAMS – SUCCESS THROUGH TRAINING AND PRACTICE

Venus Williams, a name synonymous with power, grace, and longevity in the realm of professional tennis, offers a compelling case study of how regular training and disciplined practice routines can carve a path to success. With a career that spans over two decades, Venus has not only achieved remarkable milestones but also revolutionized women's tennis with her style of play. This case study explores the training ethos and practice routines that have underpinned her illustrious career.

Early Career and Rise to Prominence

From the outset, Venus Williams was marked for greatness. Trained rigorously by her father, Richard Williams, Venus, alongside her sister Serena, was introduced to a regimented practice schedule from a young age. Her early training emphasized not just technical skills but also physical conditioning, mental toughness, and a strategic understanding of the game. This holistic approach to training laid the foundation for her future successes.

Practice Routines and Consistency

The cornerstone of Venus's success has been her unwavering commitment to regular practice and consistency in her training routines. Even at the peak of her career, Venus maintained a disciplined approach to training, understanding that continual improvement is vital to staying competitive. Her practice sessions, often conducted under the watchful eyes of her coaches and trainers, have remained intense and focused, aimed at maintaining her competitive edge.

Proactive and Comprehensive Rehabilitation

Venus's strategy for overcoming injuries includes a proactive stance toward rehabilitation. She has consistently emphasized the importance of listening to her body, seeking immediate medical advice, and following tailored rehabilitation programs. Her recovery process often involves a multidisciplinary team, including physiotherapists, fitness trainers, and medical professionals, ensuring a holistic approach to healing.

Legacy and Impact

Venus Williams's career is a testament to the power of regular training and practice in achieving and sustaining success at the highest levels of tennis. Her achievements, including seven Grand Slam singles titles and four Olympic gold medals, reflect her hard work, dedication, and relentless pursuit of excellence.

Armed with a solid training regimen that encompasses technical skills, physical conditioning, and recovery strategies, the journey toward tennis excellence doesn't halt. Mastery is an ongoing pursuit characterized by the relentless quest for improvement and the flexibility to adapt to new challenges. As we transition into Chapter 8, "The Mental Game," we'll delve into the mindset essential for sustaining a competitive edge throughout your tennis career. This chapter will explore how to develop a competitive mindset, stress management techniques, visualization, and goal setting. The legends of tennis have different playing styles, but they share one thing in common: they are mental fortresses.

THE MENTAL GAME

I n tennis, the battle is not solely across the net but also within the mind. As the great Björn Borg once said, "The key to success is self-confidence. The key to self-confidence is preparation." In Chapter 8, "The Mental Game," we unlock the secrets of mental fortitude, harnessing the power of a prepared and confident mind to conquer the psychological challenges of tennis.

MENTAL PREPARATION

Visualization and Goal Setting

Visualization and goal setting are potent tools in a tennis player's mental preparation arsenal, providing clarity, motivation, and a roadmap for success. These techniques help players mentally rehearse outcomes, stay focused on objectives, and foster a positive and proactive mindset.

Visualization Techniques

Visualization, or mental imagery, involves creating detailed mental pictures of desired outcomes and processes. This technique is not just about seeing success but also about feeling and experiencing it in your mind's eye. Here's how to effectively incorporate visualization into your mental preparation:

- **Specific Scenarios:** Visualize specific match scenarios, including playing against tough opponents, facing break points, and executing perfect shots under pressure. The more detailed the visualization, the more effective it will be in preparing you mentally for similar situations on the court.
- **Positive Outcomes:** Focus on positive outcomes, such as winning a crucial game or hitting an ace. Feel the emotions associated with these successes, such as joy and confidence, reinforcing positive associations with high-pressure moments.
- **Process Visualization:** Beyond outcomes, visualize the processes involved in playing well. Imagine yourself moving fluidly across the court, making precise contact with the ball, and employing effective strategies against different types of players.
- **Daily Practice:** Incorporate visualization into your daily routine, dedicating time before practice sessions or matches to mentally rehearse your performance. Regular practice strengthens the neural pathways associated with the visualized skills, enhancing muscle memory and confidence.

Goal Setting

Goal setting provides direction and purpose, breaking down the journey to tennis proficiency into manageable steps. Effective goal setting involves:

- **SMART Goals:** Ensure your goals are Specific, Measurable, Achievable, Relevant, and Time-Bound (SMART). For example, instead of a vague goal like "improve my serve," set a specific goal such as "increase my first serve percentage to 65% within the next three months."
- **Short-Term and Long-Term Goals:** Balance short-term objectives, such as improving a specific stroke or tactic, with long-term aspirations, like winning a local tournament or achieving a particular ranking. This balance keeps you motivated and focused on both immediate improvements and future ambitions.
- **Process and Performance Goals:** While outcome goals (e.g., winning a match) are important, focus also on process goals (e.g., maintaining a positive attitude regardless of the score) and performance goals (e.g., executing a certain number of deep returns in a match). These types of goals are within your control and directly contribute to skill development and mental resilience.
- **Review and Adjust:** Regularly review your goals to assess progress and make adjustments as needed. Celebrate achievements to reinforce success, and analyze any shortfalls to understand what changes or additional focus might be required.

Combining visualization with goal setting creates a powerful synergy that enhances mental preparation. Visualization brings goals to life, making them more tangible and attainable, while goal setting provides the structure and milestones needed to guide your visualization practice. Together, they forge a focused, confident mindset that is essential for success in the competitive world of tennis.

MENTAL TOUGHNESS AND RESILIENCE

Handling Pressure Situations

The ability to handle pressure situations effectively is a hallmark of mental toughness and resilience in tennis. Matches often come down to a few crucial points, and the outcome can hinge on a player's ability to stay composed, focused, and confident under pressure. Developing strategies to manage these high-stakes moments is essential for any player aspiring to improve their game. Here's how to approach handling pressure situations:

Embrace the Moment

- **Positive Framing:** View pressure situations as opportunities to demonstrate your skills and hard work rather than threats. Positive framing can transform anxiety into excitement and motivation.
- **Stay Present:** Focus on the here and now rather than the potential outcome of the point or match. Concentrate on your breathing, your tactics for the next point, and your pre-point routine to stay grounded in the present.

Routine Is Key

- **Develop a Consistent Pre-Point Routine:** Routines can provide a sense of control and normalcy, even in high-pressure situations. Whether it's bouncing the ball a certain number of times before serving or visualizing your shot, stick to your routine to maintain focus and calmness.
- **Mental Rehearsal:** Use visualization techniques to mentally rehearse how you will play crucial points. Visualizing successful outcomes can boost confidence and reduce nervousness when the moment arrives.

Focus on What You Can Control

- **Control the Controllables:** Concentrate on aspects of the game within your control, such as effort, attitude, and strategy. Letting go of uncontrollable factors, like the weather or an opponent's play, reduces unnecessary stress.
- **Process Over Outcome:** Focus on executing your shots and strategies rather than obsessing over the score or the possibility of winning or losing. Concentrating on the process helps maintain a clear head and reduces performance anxiety.

Breathing and Relaxation Techniques

- **Deep Breathing:** Practice deep breathing exercises to manage the physical symptoms of stress and anxiety. Deep, controlled breaths can lower your heart rate and relax muscles, helping you stay calm and collected.
- **Progressive Muscle Relaxation:** Learn to recognize when your body is tensing up during play and use progressive muscle relaxation to release this tension between points.

Build Resilience Through Practice

- **Simulate Pressure in Practice:** Create pressure situations during practice sessions, such as playing points where you must hold serve to win the set. This exposure helps normalize the feelings associated with pressure and improves your ability to perform under stress.
- **Reflect and Learn:** After matches, reflect on how you handled pressure moments, regardless of the outcome. Identify what worked well and areas for improvement. This reflection process is crucial for developing long-term mental toughness and resilience.

Handling pressure situations in tennis is as much about preparation and mindset as it is about in-the-moment tactics. By embracing pressure as an opportunity, relying on routines, focusing on controllable elements, and using relaxation techniques, players can enhance their ability to perform when it counts the most. Cultivating these mental skills through deliberate practice and reflection fosters resilience, turning pressure situations into platforms for showcasing your strongest game.

Overcoming Setbacks During a Match

Setbacks during a match, such as losing a crucial game, facing unexpected errors, or encountering a sudden shift in momentum, can test a player's mental toughness and resilience. How you respond to these challenges can significantly impact your performance and the match outcome. Developing strategies to overcome setbacks is essential for maintaining focus, confidence, and competitiveness. Here's how to approach recovering from setbacks during a match:

Acknowledge and Accept

- **Acceptance:** Recognize that setbacks are a natural part of competitive tennis. Accepting the situation without judgment allows you to move forward more effectively.
- **Short Memory:** Cultivate the ability to let go of past points or games quickly. Dwelling on mistakes or missed opportunities can hinder your focus on the present and future play.

Reframe the Situation

- **Positive Reframing:** Instead of viewing setbacks as failures, see them as challenges to overcome or opportunities to learn and grow. This mindset shift can turn adversity into a motivational force.
- **Focus on Effort and Improvement:** Concentrate on putting forth your best effort and making incremental improvements rather than fixating on the scoreboard.

Reset and Refocus

- **Use Routines:** Leverage your pre-point or pre-game routines as a mental "reset" button. These routines can help you refocus on the task at hand, leaving the setback behind.
- **Visualization:** Before resuming play, take a moment to visualize executing a successful shot or winning the next point. This mental imagery can boost confidence and clarity.

Learning From Losses

In tennis, as in all competitive sports, losses are inevitable. How a player responds to these setbacks can significantly impact their mental resilience and future performance. Viewing losses as learning opportunities rather than failures is a crucial aspect of mental preparation. This positive approach to defeat helps players grow, refine their game, and come back stronger. Here's how to effectively learn from losses:

- **Embrace a Growth Mindset:** Adopting a growth mindset means understanding that skills and abilities can be developed through dedication and hard work. When you lose a match, view it as a chance to identify areas for improvement rather than a reflection of your inherent talent or worth. This mindset encourages resilience and a proactive approach to personal development.
- **Analyze the Match Objectively:** After a loss, it's essential to analyze your performance objectively. Review the match, if possible, through video recordings, or reflect on key moments and turning points. Identify both the positive aspects of your play and the areas where you struggled. Focus on specific technical, tactical, or mental aspects rather than dwelling on the outcome.
- **Seek Constructive Feedback:** Consult with your coach, hitting partners, or even your opponent for an external perspective on your performance. Constructive feedback can provide insights that you might not have considered and can help pinpoint specific areas for improvement. This collaborative approach to analysis can also reinforce a supportive tennis community and foster a positive learning environment.

- **Set Actionable Goals for Improvement:** Based on your analysis and the feedback received, set actionable goals to address identified weaknesses. These might include technical adjustments, tactical strategies, or mental skills like concentration or stress management. Incorporating these goals into your training plan ensures focused efforts on areas that can have a significant impact on your game.

Learning from losses is a critical component of a tennis player's mental preparation. It transforms potentially negative experiences into valuable lessons that contribute to personal and athletic growth. By embracing a growth mindset, analyzing performances objectively, seeking feedback, setting actionable goals, practicing mental resilience, and celebrating progress, players can use losses as a springboard to higher levels of achievement and satisfaction in their tennis journey.

CASE STUDY: RAFAEL NADAL – MENTAL FORTITUDE MASTER

Rafael Nadal's illustrious career in tennis is a testament to his extraordinary blend of talent, strategic acumen, and unparalleled mental toughness. Known for his dominance on clay, Nadal has proven his versatility across all surfaces, achieving a rare level of success that places him among the greatest in the sport's history. This case study delves into how meticulous match preparation and his indomitable spirit have contributed to his career success.

Match Preparation & Game Plan

Nadal's approach to match preparation is both thorough and strategic, underpinning his achievements on the court. Prior to matches, he engages in a detailed analysis of his opponents, studying their play to identify patterns, strengths, and weaknesses. This rigorous preparation is evident in his ability to anticipate opponents' moves and counter them effectively, often turning their advantages into vulnerabilities.

- **Surface Adaptation:** Integral to Nadal's game plan is his ability to tailor his strategy to different surfaces. On clay, his aggressive topspin forehands push opponents back, while on hard courts, he incorporates flatter shots and serves to penetrate the court more effectively. His adaptability is a cornerstone of his strategy, allowing him to excel in diverse conditions.
- **Tactical Versatility:** Nadal's tactical versatility shines through in his strategic use of serve-and-volley plays, drop shots, and lobs to keep opponents off-balance. He excels in constructing points, using his heavy topspin to control the tempo and positioning of rallies, forcing errors, or creating openings to attack.

Mental Toughness & Resilience

Nadal's mental toughness is as legendary as his physical prowess. His ability to stay focused under pressure, maintain intensity throughout long matches, and rally from behind is unparalleled. This mental resilience has been crucial in pivotal moments, from saving match points to turning around seemingly lost causes.

- **Overcoming Challenges:** Throughout his career, Nadal has faced numerous injuries and setbacks. His resilience in overcoming these obstacles, returning stronger each time, speaks to his mental fortitude. His positive attitude and work ethic in the face of adversity have been key to his longevity and success.

- **Clutch Performance:** Nadal's performance in high-stakes moments, particularly in five-set matches and tiebreaks, underscores his psychological strength. His capacity to elevate his game when it matters most, relying on both mental and physical preparation, has led to numerous come-from-behind victories and dramatic wins.

Legacy and Impact

Rafael Nadal's career is not just a collection of titles but a legacy of how advanced strategies, mental toughness, and relentless preparation can lead to sustained excellence in professional tennis. Notably celebrated for his unprecedented dominance on clay, Nadal has captured an astounding 14 French Open titles, setting a record for the most titles won by a player at a single Grand Slam tournament. His career Grand Slam tally stands at 22 titles, a feat that places him among the elite in tennis lore, sharing the spotlight with other legends for the most Grand Slam singles titles won by a male player.

Nadal's resilience, ferocious competitive spirit, and unparalleled work ethic, combined with his sportsmanship and humility, have not only earned him a multitude of accolades but also the admiration and respect of fans and peers alike. Rafael Nadal's tennis career is a testament to his enduring legacy as a relentless competitor and a true ambassador of the sport.

Now that a strong foundation has been laid for the technical and mental aspects of the game, it's time to talk about physical improvement. As we transition into Chapter 9, "Fitness and Nutrition," we'll delve into the strategies essential for sustaining growth throughout your tennis career. This chapter will explore how to properly train and fuel your body, ensuring you remain competitive and proactive in your development. The path of continuous improvement is the hallmark of the greatest players in the sport, who understand that physical evolution is key to staying ahead and achieving lasting success.

FITNESS AND NUTRITION

In the annals of tennis history, the most revered legends are those who viewed their careers not as a journey to a fixed destination but as an endless horizon of improvement and discovery. Imagine yourself following in the footsteps of these legends— a player who, despite reaching the pinnacle of success, never stops learning, adapting, and evolving. A testament to the belief that in tennis, as in life, the quest for mastery is perpetual, and the capacity for growth knows no bounds.

As we delve into "Fitness and Nutrition," let us draw inspiration from the relentless pursuit of excellence and the transformative power of an ever-learning, ever-evolving approach to the game.

PHYSICAL PREPARATION

The Importance of Fitness in Tennis

Tennis is a sport that demands a unique blend of physical prowess, combining endurance, strength, agility, speed, and flexibility. The importance of fitness in tennis cannot be overstated; it's the foundation upon which all skills are built and executed. A well-prepared body is not only key to performing at your best but also crucial to preventing injuries that could sideline you from the game.

- **Endurance:** Tennis matches can vary greatly in length, from short sprints in a fast-paced game to marathon sessions that test the limits of human stamina. Building cardiovascular endurance is essential. It ensures you can sustain high levels of performance throughout the match, from the first serve to the final point. Endurance training, such as running, cycling, or swimming, helps improve your heart's efficiency, allowing you to maintain intense play without succumbing to fatigue.
- **Strength:** While tennis is often a game of finesse, underlying strength is what gives shots their power and depth. Core strength is particularly vital, as it stabilizes the body during swings and serves, providing the foundation for powerful shots. Leg strength enhances your ability to sprint, change direction quickly, and maintain balance. Upper body strength, especially in the shoulders, arms, and back, contributes to more forceful serves and groundstrokes. Incorporating strength training into your routine and focusing on these key areas can significantly improve your game.
- **Agility and Speed:** Tennis is a game of quick reactions. The ability to change direction swiftly, accelerate, and decelerate is what allows a player to cover the court effectively. Agility drills and speed training refine your footwork, enabling you to reach balls faster and position yourself optimally for shots. Good footwork not only

improves your defensive game but also places you in better positions to attack.

- **Flexibility:** A flexible body is more efficient on the tennis court. Improved range of motion allows for more fluid and complete swings, enhancing shot effectiveness and reducing the risk of injury. Flexibility in the shoulders, hips, and back is particularly important for serving and reaching for wide balls. Regular stretching routines, yoga, or Pilates can increase your flexibility, benefiting your game and your overall physical health.

- **Injury Prevention:** Tennis places a lot of stress on specific parts of the body, particularly the shoulders, elbows, knees, and wrists. A comprehensive fitness regime that includes endurance, strength, agility, and flexibility training not only boosts performance but also helps prevent common tennis injuries. By preparing the body for the demands of the game, you reduce the likelihood of strains, sprains, and overuse injuries that can keep you off the court.

Incorporating a balanced physical preparation plan into your tennis routine is crucial. It's not just about hitting more balls during practice; it's about building a body that can withstand the rigors of the game, execute the skills required to play well, and recover efficiently after play. As you advance in your tennis journey, your fitness level will increasingly become a significant factor in your ability to compete and enjoy the game. Remember, physical preparation is an ongoing process, evolving as you grow and develop as a player.

Basic Conditioning Exercises for Tennis Players

To excel in tennis, integrating specific conditioning exercises into your training regimen is crucial. These exercises are designed to enhance your endurance, strength, agility, and flexibility, directly translating to improved performance on the court. Here are targeted examples of conditioning exercises that cater to the physical demands of tennis:

Endurance

- **Interval Sprints:** Mimic the stop-and-start nature of tennis by alternating between sprinting and jogging. For example, sprint for 30 seconds, followed by a minute of jogging, repeating this cycle for 20–30 minutes.
- **Stair Climbing:** Find a set of stairs or stadium bleachers and run up quickly, then jog or walk down to recover. This exercise builds endurance and leg strength.
- **Long-Distance Running:** Incorporate runs of various lengths into your training regimen, ranging from 3 to 5 miles or more, depending on your fitness level. These runs build aerobic capacity, which is essential for long matches, and help improve mental toughness.
- **Cycling:** A low-impact alternative to running, cycling for 45 minutes to an hour at a moderate to vigorous intensity can significantly boost cardiovascular health and endurance. It also strengthens the leg muscles without the high impact on joints.
- **Swimming:** Swimming laps for 30 minutes to an hour provides a full-body workout that enhances cardiovascular fitness while also promoting muscle endurance. The resistance of the water adds an additional strength component to the workout.

Strength

- **Circuit Training:** Design a circuit that includes a mix of aerobic exercises and strength training, focusing on lower-body strength, core stability, and upper-body power. Exercises might include lunges, squats, push-ups, planks, and burpees, performed with minimal rest between stations. Try incorporating medicine ball throws to simulate explosive movements. This type of training simulates the varied and repetitive nature of tennis play.
- **High-Intensity Interval Training (HIIT):** HIIT sessions involve short bursts of high-intensity activity followed by brief periods of rest or low-intensity movement. For example, sprint at full effort for 30 seconds, followed by a 1-minute walk or jog for recovery, repeated for 20–30 minutes. HIIT improves both aerobic and anaerobic fitness, which is crucial for the quick, explosive movements required in tennis.

Agility

- **Side-to-Side Shuffles:** Set up cones or markers about 10 feet apart. Shuffle quickly from one to the other, staying low and touching the cone or marker at each end. This drill improves lateral movement speed.
- **T-Drill:** Set up cones in a T-shape. Sprint forward to the first cone, side shuffle to the right, then to the left, and backpedal to the start. This drill enhances agility and quick directional changes.
- **Four-Corner Drill:** Place four cones in a square layout, each approximately 10–15 feet apart. Start at one cone and sprint to the next, then shuffle sideways to the third cone, backpedal to the fourth, and shuffle sideways back to the

start. This drill improves forward, lateral, and backward movement agility.

- **Ladder Drills:** Using an agility ladder, perform various footwork patterns to enhance quickness and foot speed. Examples include the in-out drill (stepping in and out of each box with both feet), the lateral feet drill (moving sideways through the ladder with quick, short steps), and the hopscotch drill (jumping in and out of boxes with alternating feet).
- **Cone Zig-Zag Drill:** Set up cones in a zig-zag formation, each cone about 5 feet apart. Starting at the first cone, sprint to the next, planting your outside foot to change direction quickly, weaving through the cones. This drill helps improve quick pivots and directional changes.

Flexibility

- **Dynamic Stretching Routine:** Before playing or practicing, perform dynamic stretches to prepare your muscles and joints. Include leg swings (front-to-back and side-to-side), arm circles, and torso twists. These movements should be fluid and controlled, gradually increasing in range as your muscles warm up.
- **Yoga for Tennis Players:** Yoga can be incredibly beneficial for tennis players, focusing on poses that enhance flexibility, balance, and core strength. Poses such as the pigeon pose for hip flexibility, the warrior series for leg and ankle strength, and the cobra pose for spinal flexibility are particularly beneficial.
- **Post-Play Stretching:** After playing, it's essential to cool down with static stretching to relax the muscles and improve flexibility over time. Focus on stretches that

target the shoulders, back, hamstrings, quadriceps, calves, and forearms, holding each stretch for at least 30 seconds.

Speed

- **Suicide Drills:** Mark several lines or spots on the court or field, each progressively further from the starting point. Sprint to the first mark, touch the ground, sprint back to the start, and then out to the second mark, continuing until all marks have been reached. This drill improves speed, endurance, and agility.

Incorporating these conditioning exercises into your routine several times a week can significantly enhance your physical capabilities on the tennis court. Tailor the intensity and volume of the exercises to your fitness level and tennis goals, and consider consulting with a coach or fitness professional to ensure proper form and maximize benefits while minimizing the risk of injury.

NUTRITION AND HYDRATION

Essential Nutrition for Tennis Players

Proper nutrition is crucial for tennis players to perform at their best, recover quickly, and maintain overall health. A balanced diet that meets the demands of training, matches, and recovery can significantly impact a player's energy levels, endurance, concentration, and injury prevention. Here's a breakdown of essential nutrition components for tennis players:

Carbohydrates

- Carbohydrates are the primary energy source for tennis players, especially important given the sport's stop-and-start nature and the need for bursts of explosive energy.
- Include complex carbohydrates like whole grains, fruits, vegetables, and legumes in your diet to provide a steady energy supply. Prior to matches or intense training sessions, easily digestible carbohydrates (e.g., bananas or sports drinks) can provide a quick energy boost.

Proteins

- Proteins are essential for muscle repair and recovery and are particularly important in a physically demanding sport like tennis.
- Incorporate a variety of protein sources, including lean meats, fish, dairy products, eggs, and plant-based options like tofu, lentils, and quinoa, to support muscle health and recovery.

Fats

- While often misunderstood, healthy fats are a vital energy source for long-duration activities and support cell function and nutrient absorption.
- Focus on unsaturated fats found in foods like avocados, nuts, seeds, olive oil, and fatty fish (such as salmon and mackerel) to promote energy and overall health.

Hydration

- Staying well-hydrated is essential for optimal performance and health. Dehydration can lead to fatigue, decreased coordination, and muscle cramps, severely impacting a player's ability to compete.
- Drink water consistently throughout the day, and increase intake before, during, and after training or matches. Electrolyte-replenishing drinks can be beneficial during extended play, especially in hot conditions.

Micronutrients

- Vitamins and minerals support various bodily functions, including energy production, bone health, and immune function.
- Ensure a diet rich in a variety of fruits, vegetables, whole grains, and lean proteins to meet micronutrient needs. Specific nutrients to focus on include calcium and vitamin D for bone health, iron for energy metabolism and oxygen transport, and antioxidants (such as vitamins C and E) to help combat oxidative stress from intense physical activity.

Pre- and Post-Exercise Nutrition

- Pre-exercise meals or snacks should focus on carbohydrates for energy and a small amount of protein to aid muscle function.
- Post-exercise nutrition is critical for recovery, emphasizing protein to repair muscles and carbohydrates to replenish glycogen stores. A meal or snack within 30 minutes to two hours after training or competition can optimize recovery.

A well-planned nutrition strategy tailored to the individual needs of a tennis player can enhance performance, support recovery, and contribute to long-term health and success in the sport. Consulting with a sports nutritionist can provide personalized recommendations based on training intensity, competition schedule, and individual health needs.

Hydration Strategies

Hydration is a critical component of a tennis player's nutrition plan, significantly affecting performance, endurance, and recovery. Proper hydration strategies help maintain concentration, prevent cramps and injuries, and ensure the body functions optimally, especially during long matches or in hot conditions. Here are key hydration strategies for tennis players:

Understand Your Hydration Needs

- Every athlete's hydration needs are unique and can be influenced by factors such as body size, sweat rate, climate, and the intensity of play. It's important to monitor your individual hydration status by paying attention to thirst cues, urine color (aim for pale yellow), and changes in body weight before and after playing.

Pre-Hydration

- Begin matches and training sessions well-hydrated. Drink approximately 17–20 ounces (500–600 ml) of water 2–3 hours before starting, followed by an additional 8 ounces (about 240 ml) 20–30 minutes before play. Pre-hydration ensures you start at an optimal hydration level, which is particularly important for long sessions or competitions.

Hydrate During Play

- Drink regularly throughout practice and matches to replace fluids lost through sweat. A general guideline is to consume 7–10 ounces (about 200–300 ml) every 10–20 minutes of play, but this can vary based on individual needs and conditions.
- In hot and humid conditions, consider sports drinks that contain electrolytes (particularly sodium and potassium) to replace what is lost in sweat and aid in hydration absorption. Electrolytes help maintain fluid balance and prevent hyponatremia, a condition resulting from low sodium levels.

Post-Exercise Rehydration

- Rehydrating after play is crucial for recovery, especially if you have another training session or match soon. Aim to replace 150% of the fluid lost during play over the next 2–4 hours. For example, if you lose 2 pounds (about 32 ounces) during play, aim to consume 48 ounces of fluid post-match.
- Including a small amount of sodium in your post-exercise beverage or meal can help expedite rehydration by stimulating thirst and retaining the consumed fluids.

Monitor and Adjust

- Hydration needs can vary greatly from day to day and under different environmental conditions. It's essential to monitor your body's responses and adjust your hydration plan accordingly.

- Be aware of signs of dehydration, including thirst, dry mouth, fatigue, decreased urine output, and dark-colored urine. Equally, be cautious of overhydration, which can lead to hyponatremia.

Plan for Conditions

- Anticipate the weather conditions and plan your hydration strategy accordingly. Hotter, more humid conditions will increase sweat rates and fluid needs. Conversely, cooler weather might reduce the perceived need to drink, but hydration remains critical.

Incorporating these hydration strategies into your training and competition routines can significantly impact your performance and well-being on the court. Regularly assessing and adjusting your hydration practices will help you stay at the top of your game, regardless of the conditions.

Pre- and Post-Match Eating

Effective nutritional strategies surrounding match play are crucial for maximizing performance on the court and ensuring efficient recovery afterward. Here's how tennis players can optimize their pre- and post-match eating to support energy levels, stamina, and recovery processes.

Pre-Match Eating

The goal of pre-match nutrition is to fuel your body with the energy it needs to perform at its best while ensuring comfort and preventing gastrointestinal distress.

- **Timing:** Consume your main meal 3–4 hours before the match. This meal should be high in carbohydrates, moderate in protein, and low in fat and fiber to facilitate digestion and minimize the risk of gastrointestinal discomfort.
- **Meal Ideas:** Suitable meals might include a plate of whole-grain pasta with a lean protein source (like chicken or tofu) and a low-fiber sauce, a turkey or hummus wrap with a side of fruit, or a large rice bowl with vegetables and grilled fish.
- **Hydration:** Begin hydrating several hours before the match, aiming to consume 17–20 ounces (about 500–600 ml) of water 2–3 hours before starting, followed by another 8 ounces (approximately 240 ml) 20–30 minutes before play.
- **Last-Minute Snacks:** If you need an energy boost closer to match time, opt for a small, carbohydrate-rich snack 30–60 minutes beforehand. Good options include a banana, a small energy bar, or a piece of toast with jam.

Post-Match Eating

Recovery starts as soon as you step off the court, with the first 30–60 minutes post-exercise being a critical window for replenishing energy stores and beginning the muscle repair process.

- **Immediate Recovery Snack:** Aim to consume a mix of carbohydrates and protein shortly after the match to kickstart the recovery process. A ratio of 3:1 (carbohydrates to protein) is often recommended. Suitable snacks might include a protein shake with fruit, a yogurt parfait with granola, or a peanut butter and jelly sandwich.

- **Hydration:** Replace fluids lost during play by drinking water or an electrolyte-replenishing beverage. Continue hydrating until the urine is pale yellow, indicating proper rehydration.
- **Recovery Meal:** Within 2–4 hours of your match, have a balanced meal containing carbohydrates, protein, and fats to further aid in recovery. Examples include a quinoa salad with roasted vegetables and grilled salmon or chicken stir-fry with brown rice and assorted vegetables.
- **Considerations for Multiple Matches in a Day:** If you have multiple matches or sessions in a day, focus on rapidly digestible carbohydrates and moderate protein intake between matches to replenish glycogen stores and support muscle recovery. Maintain hydration and electrolyte balance with water and sports drinks.

Tailoring your pre and post-match nutrition can significantly affect energy levels, performance, and recovery. Experiment with different foods and timing to find what works best for your body and schedule, keeping in mind that nutritional needs can vary based on the duration, intensity of play, and individual health and dietary requirements.

CASE STUDY – SERENA WILLIAMS' PREPARATION FOR TENNIS

Serena Williams, one of the most formidable athletes in tennis history, exemplifies what it means to prepare comprehensively for the sport. Her approach to physical conditioning, mental fortitude, nutrition, and hydration underscores the holistic preparation required to compete at the highest levels. This case study delves into how Serena prepares to dominate on the tennis court.

Physical Preparation

Comprehensive Training Regime

- Serena's physical preparation extends beyond the tennis court, incorporating cardiovascular conditioning, strength training, and flexibility exercises. Her routine includes running, cycling, and swimming to build endurance, coupled with weightlifting sessions that focus on both upper and lower body strength—key to generating power behind her serves and groundstrokes.
- On-court practice is meticulously planned, focusing on improving her already formidable skills, with particular attention to serve accuracy and return agility. Drills are designed to simulate match conditions, ensuring that Serena is ready for the physical demands of competitive play.

Injury Prevention and Recovery

- Understanding the importance of recovery, Serena incorporates yoga and Pilates into her routine to enhance flexibility and reduce the risk of injury. Regular physiotherapy sessions, including massage and cryotherapy, are integral to her regimen, aiding in muscle recovery and injury prevention.

Mental Preparation

Visualization and Strategy

- Serena employs visualization techniques, imagining various match scenarios and her responses to them. This mental rehearsal helps enhance her focus and decision-making on the court.

- Her preparation also involves studying opponents' games and strategizing with her coach to devise game plans that play to her strengths while exploiting opponents' weaknesses.

Psychological Resilience

- Serena's mental toughness is legendary. She works closely with a sports psychologist to develop coping strategies for high-pressure situations, ensuring she remains composed and competitive regardless of the scoreline.
- Her preparation includes exercises in mindfulness and meditation, which help maintain concentration during matches and manage the stress and expectations of professional competition.

Nutrition and Hydration Preparation

Tailored Nutrition Plan

- Serena follows a tailored nutrition plan that supports her training demands, emphasizing lean proteins, whole grains, and plenty of fruits and vegetables to provide the necessary vitamins and minerals for energy and recovery.
- Her diet is carefully balanced to optimize performance, with adjustments made based on the day's training intensity and the climatic conditions of upcoming tournaments.

Hydration Strategy

- Understanding the role of hydration in performance, Serena prioritizes maintaining electrolyte balance, especially during intense matches and in hot conditions. Her hydration strategy includes water and electrolyte-replenishing drinks to prevent dehydration and maintain optimum performance levels.
- Nutritionists and fitness coaches play a crucial role in monitoring her hydration levels and adjusting her intake as necessary to ensure she is always at her peak.

Serena Williams' preparation for tennis is a testament to her dedication and professionalism, highlighting the importance of a holistic approach to training. Her meticulous attention to physical conditioning, mental fortitude, nutrition, and hydration not only prepares her for the demands of professional tennis but also contributes to her longevity in the sport. Serena's comprehensive preparation routine serves as a blueprint for aspiring tennis players aiming for success at the highest levels.

As we approach the end of our journey through the intricacies of tennis, from mastering the fundamentals to adapting to the evolving landscape of the game, it's time to reflect on how far you've come and where you're headed. The path to tennis excellence is not solely about perfecting your forehand or strategizing your way through matches; it's also about embracing the tennis lifestyle—a commitment that extends beyond the court.

In Chapter 10, "Beyond the Basics – Embracing the Tennis Lifestyle," we'll explore the broader aspects of being a tennis player, including the culture, community, and lifelong learning that the sport offers. This final chapter is about fully immersing yourself in the world of tennis, understanding its impact on your life, and recognizing how it shapes your identity, relationships, and personal growth. Let's venture into the comprehensive embrace of tennis, not just as a sport but as a way of life.

BEYOND THE BASICS – EMBRACING THE TENNIS LIFESTYLE

T ennis is more than a game of strokes, points, and matches—it's a journey that transforms individuals in profound and lasting ways. Beyond the physical rallies lies a deeper narrative of personal growth, community, and a passion that transcends the boundaries of the court. As we explore the myriad ways tennis enriches the lives of its enthusiasts, we invite you to see the sport as a companion on your journey of personal and communal discovery.

In "Beyond the Basics – Embracing the Tennis Lifestyle," we delve into the life-changing impact tennis has on those who welcome it into their lives.

TENNIS AS A LIFELONG SPORT

Tennis stands out as a sport not just for the intensity and excitement it brings to players and fans alike but also for its unique quality as a lifelong sport. It is one of the few athletic endeavors that people can engage in from childhood through their senior years, offering not just a form of exercise but a passion that enriches life across its various stages. The following explores the health benefits of playing tennis, illustrating why it's an excellent choice for anyone seeking a sport for life.

The Health Benefits of Playing Tennis

Cardiovascular Fitness

- **Endurance and Heart Health:** Tennis is an exceptional cardiovascular workout involving short bursts of sprinting, quick movements, and endurance. Regular play improves heart health and increases cardiovascular fitness, reducing the risk of heart disease, high blood pressure, and stroke.

Full Body Workout

- **Strength and Tone:** Unlike some sports that concentrate on specific body areas, tennis engages muscles throughout the body. From the legs used for running and lunging to the arms and shoulders used for swinging the racket, tennis helps in building strength and toning muscles.
- **Core Stability:** Playing tennis regularly strengthens the core muscles, improving balance, posture, and overall stability, which are beneficial not just on the court but in daily activities.

Hand-Eye Coordination and Agility

- **Improved Coordination:** Tennis requires precise hand-eye coordination, enhancing neural connections related to timing, coordination, and spatial awareness.

- **Increased Agility:** The quick changes of direction required in tennis improve agility, reflexes, and flexibility, reducing the risk of injuries in other physical activities and daily life.

Mental Health Benefits

- **Stress Reduction:** Physical activity, including tennis, releases endorphins, the body's natural mood lifters, helping to decrease stress, alleviate anxiety, and combat depression.
- **Cognitive Benefits:** Tennis necessitates strategic thinking and on-the-spot problem-solving, fostering mental alertness and tactical thinking that can protect against cognitive decline in later years.

Social Interaction and Community

- **Building Connections:** Tennis often involves doubles play, leagues, and social gatherings, providing opportunities for social interaction and forming friendships. The tennis community offers a sense of belonging and support that can enhance emotional well-being.
- **Family Involvement:** As a sport that people of all ages can play, tennis provides a unique opportunity for family bonding and intergenerational play, strengthening family ties and encouraging a healthy, active lifestyle.

Weight Management and Bone Health

- **Calorie Burn:** Tennis is an effective way to burn calories, aiding in weight management and obesity prevention.

- **Stronger Bones:** The weight-bearing nature of tennis helps in maintaining bone density and strength, reducing the risk of osteoporosis and fractures.

Lifelong Playability and Adaptability

- **Accessibility:** Tennis can be adapted for any skill level and age, with modifications such as softer balls, smaller courts, and lighter rackets available for juniors, beginners, or senior players.
- **Injury Prevention:** With proper coaching, conditioning, and the use of appropriate equipment, tennis is a relatively low-risk sport for injuries, contributing to its sustainability as a lifelong sport.

Embracing tennis as a lifelong sport offers extensive health benefits, from physical fitness and mental sharpness to social well-being and family engagement. Its adaptability, combined with the myriad health advantages, makes tennis not just a sport to play but a lifestyle to live, enhancing the quality of life for players of all ages.

Tennis for Socializing and Networking

Beyond its physical and mental health benefits, tennis shines as a powerful medium for socializing and networking. The sport's inherent social nature fosters connections, builds communities, and opens doors to personal and professional opportunities. Whether through casual weekend matches, club leagues, or competitive tournaments, tennis provides a unique environment for meeting new people and strengthening bonds. Here's how tennis can enhance your social and networking life:

Building a Community

- **Clubs and Leagues:** Joining a tennis club or participating in local leagues offers a sense of belonging to a community with shared interests. These settings provide regular opportunities to interact with fellow tennis enthusiasts, fostering friendships and a supportive network.
- **Social Events:** Many tennis communities organize social events, mixers, and charity tournaments, which are great for socializing in a relaxed, fun environment. These events can lead to lasting friendships and connections.

Family and Interpersonal Relationships

- **Family Bonding:** Tennis is a sport that families can enjoy together, offering a fun way to spend quality time and build shared experiences. It's an activity that parents, children, and even grandparents can participate in, strengthening family bonds.
- **Teamwork and Partnerships:** Doubles play requires communication, teamwork, and trust, mirroring many interpersonal dynamics. Playing doubles with friends, family, or colleagues can enhance these relationships and develop new levels of cooperation and understanding.

Professional Networking

- **Business Leagues and Charity Events:** Tennis events often attract professionals from various industries, making them excellent venues for networking. Participating in business leagues or charity events can lead to meaningful professional connections and opportunities.

- **Shared Interest as a Conversation Starter:** Tennis serves as a common interest that can break the ice in professional settings. Conversations about favorite players, recent matches, or personal tennis experiences can lead to deeper discussions and connections.

Cultural Exchange and Global Networking

- **International Community:** Tennis is a global sport, and engaging with it can connect you to an international community of players and fans. This can lead to cultural exchanges, learning opportunities, and friendships that span across borders.
- **Travel and Tournaments:** Traveling to play in tournaments or to attend major events like the Grand Slams can expand your social and professional network on a global scale, introducing you to a diverse group of people with a common passion for tennis.

Lifelong Friendships

- **Durability of Tennis Relationships:** The friendships and connections made through tennis often last a lifetime. The shared experiences of practice, competition, and social events create strong bonds that endure beyond the court.
- **Support System:** The tennis community can provide a valuable support system, offering encouragement during challenges, celebrating successes, and providing motivation to improve both on and off the court.

Tennis transcends the physical boundaries of the court, offering a platform for socializing, networking, and building communities. Its ability to connect individuals through a shared passion makes tennis not just a sport but a catalyst for forming meaningful relationships and expanding professional networks. Whether you're seeking to enhance your social life, build professional connections, or simply enjoy the company of fellow tennis enthusiasts, the tennis lifestyle offers abundant opportunities for enriching your social and networking endeavors.

Opportunities in Competitive Tennis

Engaging in competitive tennis opens up a world of opportunities beyond personal achievement and fitness. It can serve as a gateway to scholarships, coaching careers, and even business ventures within the sports industry. Competitive play not only sharpens your skills but also expands your horizons, offering pathways to both personal and professional growth. Here's how delving into competitive tennis can enrich your life:

College Scholarships and Educational Opportunities

- **Athletic Scholarships:** For talented young players, competitive tennis can lead to athletic scholarships at colleges and universities, offering a route to higher education that might otherwise be inaccessible. It's a reward for dedication and excellence on the court that also values academic achievement.
- **College Networks:** Playing tennis at the collegiate level introduces you to a network of players, coaches, and alumni who can provide support and opportunities well beyond your college years, including career advice and job opportunities.

Career Paths in Tennis and Sports

- **Coaching and Mentoring:** Competitive experience is invaluable for a career in coaching or mentoring, providing insights into the game that can be passed on to the next generation of players. Many competitive players transition into coaching, finding it a rewarding way to share their love for the sport.
- **Sports Management and Administration:** For those interested in the business side of sports, competitive tennis offers insights into tournament organization, club management, and sports marketing. These experiences can pave the way for careers in sports management, event organization, and beyond.

Networking and Professional Development

- **Industry Connections:** The competitive tennis circuit— whether at the junior, collegiate, or professional level—is a melting pot of individuals involved in various aspects of sports, offering a rich environment for networking.
- **Skill Transfer:** The discipline, strategic thinking, and resilience developed through competitive tennis are highly valued in the professional world. These transferable skills can enhance your career, regardless of the field.

Personal Growth and Life Skills

- **Resilience and Perseverance:** The challenges of competitive tennis teach resilience and perseverance, qualities that are invaluable in personal and professional contexts.

- **Time Management and Discipline:** Balancing training, competition, and other life responsibilities requires exceptional time management and discipline, skills that contribute to success in any endeavor.

Expanding Your Global Perspective

- **Travel and Cultural Exchange:** Competitive tennis often involves traveling to tournaments in different regions or countries, offering unique opportunities for cultural exchange and broadening your global perspective.
- **International Competitiveness:** Competing internationally exposes you to different playing styles and strategies, enhancing your adaptability and understanding of the global game.

Lifelong Competitiveness and Fitness

- **Sustained Physical Activity:** Competitive play encourages a lifelong commitment to physical fitness and health.
- **Veteran and Senior Competitions:** Tennis offers competitive outlets at all ages, from junior circuits to senior tournaments, ensuring that the competitive spirit can be maintained throughout your life.

Embracing competitive tennis provides more than the thrill of the game; it opens doors to educational opportunities, career paths, and personal growth. Whether you aspire to collegiate success, a professional career in tennis or sports management, or simply seek the personal development that comes from competitive challenges, the world of competitive tennis offers a rich and rewarding landscape to explore.

GIVING BACK TO THE TENNIS COMMUNITY

A profound aspect of embracing the tennis lifestyle is recognizing the importance of giving back to the community that fosters one's growth and passion for the game. As players evolve, many find fulfillment and purpose in contributing to the development of others and the sport itself. This section delves into the impactful roles of volunteering and coaching, highlighting how these activities not only benefit the tennis community but also enrich the personal and professional lives of those who participate.

Volunteering and Coaching

The Value of Volunteering

- **Community Development:** Volunteers play a crucial role in organizing local tournaments, running community tennis programs, and maintaining facilities. These efforts ensure that tennis remains accessible and enjoyable for all, promoting the sport's growth at the grassroots level.
- **Youth Engagement:** Volunteering in youth tennis initiatives can have a transformative impact on the lives of young players, providing them with guidance, mentorship, and opportunities to pursue their tennis aspirations.
- **Personal Satisfaction:** Beyond the tangible benefits to the community, volunteering offers a sense of fulfillment and connection, fostering a deep sense of belonging within the tennis ecosystem.

The Role of Coaching

- **Skill Development:** Coaches are instrumental in developing players' technical, tactical, and mental skills. By giving back through coaching, experienced players can share their knowledge and insights, helping others navigate the challenges and triumphs of the sport.

- **Mentorship:** Coaching goes beyond teaching strokes and strategies; it involves mentoring players and instilling values such as discipline, sportsmanship, and resilience. This mentorship can profoundly influence players' lives, both on and off the court.
- **Career Pathways:** For those passionate about tennis, coaching offers a rewarding career path that allows for continued involvement in the sport while fostering the next generation of players. It's an avenue to stay connected to tennis, evolving with the game and contributing to its future.

Building a Supportive Environment

- **Fostering Inclusivity:** Volunteers and coaches play a key role in creating an inclusive environment that welcomes players from all backgrounds and skill levels. By promoting diversity and accessibility, they ensure that tennis is a sport for everyone.
- **Encouraging Lifelong Participation:** Through their dedication, volunteers and coaches encourage players to see tennis as a lifelong sport, one that offers continuous opportunities for growth, health, and camaraderie.

Professional and Personal Growth

- **Leadership Skills:** Volunteering and coaching develop leadership skills, including communication, organization, and problem-solving. These skills are valuable in any professional context, enhancing career prospects and personal development.

- **Networking:** Engaging in these roles expands your network within the tennis community and beyond, opening doors to new opportunities and connections.

Contributing to the Legacy of Tennis

- **Sustaining the Sport's Future:** By giving back, volunteers and coaches contribute to the sustainability and evolution of tennis, ensuring that future generations can enjoy and benefit from the sport as much as they have.

Volunteering and coaching in the tennis community are powerful ways to give back, enriching the sport and its players while offering personal fulfillment and growth. These roles embody the spirit of the tennis lifestyle, highlighting the interconnectedness of personal achievement, community development, and the enduring love of the game.

SETTING NEW GOALS

As players deepen their engagement with tennis, transitioning from mastering the basics to fully immersing themselves in the sport's lifestyle, the horizon of possibilities expands. This journey opens up opportunities to dream bigger and set new, more ambitious goals. Beyond the basics, setting new goals is about challenging yourself, exploring uncharted territories in your tennis journey, and striving for continuous improvement and fulfillment both on and off the court.

Dreaming Bigger: Beyond the Basics

Elevating Performance Goals

- **Higher Competitive Levels:** Aim to compete at higher levels, whether moving up in local leagues, participating in regional tournaments, or setting sights on national competitions. Each step up represents not just a leap in competition but also personal growth and achievement.
- **Skill Mastery and Expansion:** Set goals around mastering specific aspects of your game that you've identified as weaknesses or exploring entirely new techniques and strategies. This could involve developing a more powerful serve, improving your net play, or integrating advanced footwork into your game.

Dreaming bigger and setting new goals beyond the basics of tennis encourages players to continually evolve, pushing the boundaries of what they can achieve both on and off the court. It's about embracing the full spectrum of opportunities that tennis offers for personal growth, community engagement, and lifelong fulfillment.

CASE STUDY: ROGER FEDERER – ACHIEVING CAREER GOALS AND GIVING BACK TO TENNIS

Roger Federer, whose name is synonymous with grace, excellence, and sportsmanship, has not only achieved monumental career goals but has also significantly contributed to the sport of tennis, leaving a lasting legacy. Federer's journey from a talented youngster with a fiery temper to one of the greatest ambassadors of tennis illustrates a remarkable evolution marked by achievement, resilience, and philanthropy.

Achieving Career Goals

- **Grand Slam Victories:** Federer's quest for excellence saw him capturing 20 Grand Slam singles titles, a record at the time, including a historic eight Wimbledon titles, solidifying his reputation as one of the greatest players ever to grace the sport.
- **World No. 1:** Federer held the ATP No. 1 spot in the rankings for a record total of 310 weeks, including a record 237 consecutive weeks, showcasing his dominance and consistency at the highest level of the game.
- **Pioneering Achievements:** Among his myriad achievements, Federer completed a career Grand Slam by winning all four major titles and winning a gold medal in doubles at the 2008 Beijing Olympics and a silver in singles at the 2012 London Olympics, further cementing his legacy.

Overcoming Challenges

- Federer faced significant challenges throughout his career, including battling against the younger generation of players and overcoming injuries. His ability to adapt his game, embrace new strategies, and maintain a high level of fitness contributed to his longevity and success.

Giving Back to Tennis

- **The Roger Federer Foundation:** Established in 2003, the foundation focuses on improving educational outcomes for children in Southern Africa and Switzerland. Federer's commitment to philanthropy reflects his understanding of the role that education plays in empowerment and his desire to use his success to make a positive impact.

- **Promoting the Sport:** Beyond his foundation, Federer has been instrumental in promoting tennis globally, participating in charity matches, supporting player initiatives, and engaging with fans in a way that has brought the sport to new audiences.
- **Sportsmanship and Mentorship:** Federer's demeanor on and off the court has set a benchmark for sportsmanship. His respect for competitors, graciousness in victory and defeat, and willingness to mentor younger players have endeared him to fans and peers alike, promoting a positive culture within the sport.

Legacy

- Federer's legacy is not defined solely by his records but also by the manner in which he achieved his success and gave back to the sport. His impact extends beyond the court, embodying the ideals of excellence, integrity, and generosity.
- As Federer transitions to the next phase of his life following his retirement from professional tennis, his influence continues through his philanthropic efforts, his promotion of tennis, and his role as a global ambassador for the sport.

Roger Federer's career encapsulates the journey of a sportsman who not only reached the pinnacle of success through talent and hard work but also utilized his platform to contribute positively to the world. His legacy, characterized by monumental achievements, overcoming adversity, and a profound commitment to giving back, ensures that Federer's impact on tennis and beyond will be felt for generations to come.

As we close this chapter on setting new goals and dreaming bigger, it's important to remember that your tennis journey is just beginning. The stories shared, the strategies outlined, and the inspiration drawn from those who've walked this path before you serve as a foundation for what lies ahead. Tennis is not just a game of physical prowess but a lifelong endeavor that challenges the mind, builds character, and connects us with a community of like-minded individuals. As we transition to the conclusion of this guide, carry forward the lessons learned, the aspirations kindled, and the determination to continuously evolve. Your journey in tennis is a reflection of your journey in life—rich with opportunities for growth, fulfillment, and the joy of chasing after your dreams. Let's step into the future of your tennis journey with enthusiasm, resilience, and an open heart, ready to embrace all the adventures that await.

CONCLUSION

As we reach the conclusion of this guide, it's time to reflect on the journey we've embarked upon together. From the initial steps onto the court, mastering the basics, to setting new goals and embracing the tennis lifestyle, each chapter has been a step forward in your tennis journey. But remember, this journey is far from over; it's an ongoing adventure that promises growth, challenges, and fulfillment.

REFLECTING ON THE JOURNEY

Throughout this guide, we've explored the multifaceted world of tennis—a sport that tests our limits and teaches us about resilience, discipline, and the joy of continuous improvement. Key lessons have spanned from developing a solid foundation in the basics of the game to understanding the importance of mental toughness, from the strategies that elevate our play to the lifelong benefits that come from engaging with the tennis community. Each section has not only aimed to enhance your skills on the court but also to deepen your love for the game.

The progress you've made is a testament to your commitment and passion for tennis. Whether you've refined your serve, improved your footwork, or become more mentally resilient, each step forward is a building block for future success. Remember, progress in tennis is not always linear. It's characterized by peaks and valleys, victories and setbacks, but every experience contributes to your growth as a player and a person.

LOOKING AHEAD

As you look ahead, let the horizon of your tennis journey be broad and ambitious. Continue practicing with purpose, seeking out new challenges, and embracing opportunities for learning and growth. The path to excellence in tennis is paved with dedication, continuous practice, and the relentless pursuit of improvement. Set your sights on new goals, whether they involve competitive achievements, mastering new techniques, or contributing to the tennis community.

Stay curious and open-minded, always willing to learn from coaches, peers, and even opponents. Each match, practice session, and interaction is an opportunity to learn something new. The tennis journey is enriched by the people we meet and the experiences we share, creating a tapestry of memories that last a lifetime.

THE IMPORTANCE OF PASSION

At the heart of your tennis journey is passion—the ultimate driver of success. It's your love for the game that will motivate you to hit one more ball, play one more match, and push through challenges. Passion fuels your commitment, lights up your competitive spirit, and sustains your engagement with tennis through the highs and lows.

Nurture this passion by remembering why you fell in love with tennis in the first place. Whether it's the thrill of competition, the satisfaction of personal achievement, or the joy of being part of a community, let these elements keep your passion alive. Celebrate your successes, learn from your failures, and always keep the flame of your love for the game burning brightly.

FINAL WORDS OF MOTIVATION

As we conclude this guide, take a moment to acknowledge how far you've come and the limitless potential that lies ahead. Your tennis journey is uniquely yours, defined not just by trophies or rankings but also by the courage to chase your dreams, the resilience to overcome obstacles, and the willingness to put in the work day after day.

Remember, greatness in tennis isn't just about what you achieve on the court; it's also about the character you build, the lives you touch, and the legacy you leave behind. As you continue on your path, carry with you the lessons learned, the friendships forged, and the joy that tennis brings into your life.

Let these words serve as your rallying cry: Believe in yourself, embrace the journey, and pursue your tennis goals with confidence and determination. The court is not just a battleground; it's a stage for showcasing your passion, talent, and spirit. Stand ready to write the next chapter of your tennis story—one that's filled with achievement, growth, and the sheer love of the game.

In the end, tennis is more than a sport—it's a way of life that offers endless opportunities for discovery, fulfillment, and happiness. Here's to the many matches ahead, the challenges to be faced, and the victories to be celebrated. May your tennis journey be long, rewarding, and, above all, enjoyed to the fullest. Keep playing, keep learning, and keep loving the game.

A BEGINNER'S GUIDE TO TENNIS

"When we share our love for the game, we give joy to others. Paying it forward, one racket at a time."

— UNKNOWN

Now you have everything you need to master the game of tennis, it's time to pass on your newfound knowledge and show other readers where they can find the same help.

Simply by leaving your honest opinion of this book on Amazon, you'll show other tennis enthusiasts where they can find the information they're looking for, and pass their passion for tennis forward.

Thank you for your help. The game of tennis is kept alive when we pass on our knowledge – and you're helping me to do just that.

Please help tennis players around the world by leaving this book a review.

Simply scan the QR code below to leave your review:

Thank you for your support.

Your biggest fan,

- Derek Drozd

PS - Fun fact: If you provide something of value to another person, it makes you more valuable to them. If you'd like goodwill straight from another tennis player - and you believe this book will help them - send this book their way.

REFERENCES

Foster Wallace, D. (n.d.). String theory: David Foster Wallace on tennis. *Library of America*. https://www.loa.org/books/504-string-theory-david-foster-wallace-on-tennis/

Gallwey, T. W. (2024, April 12). *The Inner Game of Tennis*. Penguin Random House Higher Education. https://penguinrandomhousehighereducation.com/book/?isbn=9780679778318

Gilbert, B., & Jamison, S. (1994). *Winning ugly: Mental warfare in tennis--lessons from a master* (1st Fireside ed.). Simon & Schuster.

Group, S. B. (2024, April 4). *Watch tennis channel and tennis channel plus*. Tennis Channel. https://tennischannel.com/tennischannel.com

Karue, S. (n.d.). *My tennis hq-Youtube*. https://www.youtube.com/@MyTennisHQ

Nadal, R., & Carlin, J. (2012). *Rafa: My story*. Sphere. https://www.amazon.com/Rafa-My-Story-Rafael-Nadal/dp/0751547735

Playing tennis. (2022, November 27). Tennis Frontier Forums. https://www.tennisfrontier.com/forums/playing-tennis-forum/

R/tennis. (n.d.). Reddit. https://www.reddit.com/r/tennis/

Salzenstein, J. (n.d.). *Tennis evolution* [YouTube]. Tennis Evolution. https://www.youtube.com/@TennisEvolution

Talk tennis. (2018, November 3). Tennis Warehouse. https://tt.tennis-warehouse.com/index.php

Top tennis training—Pro tennis lessons. (n.d.). [YouTube]. Top Tennis Training. https://www.youtube.com/@TopTennisTrainingOfficial

TopCourt. (n.d.). [YouTube]. TopCourt. https://www.youtube.com/c/topcourt

Welcome to Our Tennis Community. (2024, May 7). Tennis Frontier Forums. https://tennisfrontier.com/

Williams, S., & Paisner, D. (2010). *My life: Queen of the court*. Simon & Schuster Ltd. https://www.amazon.com/My-Life-Queen-Serena-Williams/dp/1847396453#detailBullets_feature_div

Printed in Great Britain
by Amazon

51115366R00136